REAL GARDENS

By ADAM FROST

Seven amazing Chelsea Gold Medal-winning Designs

Chelsea Gold Medal Gardens

Foreword

By David Stevens FSGD, FCI Hort

To choose landscaping as a career is not an easy option. It's a multi-faceted vocation that demands an understanding of horticulture, construction, design and above all people. To create a successful garden involves far more than painting a pretty picture. The problem with this ever-growing sector of the design market is that many practitioners have little idea of the practicalities of how a delicate space is put together.

There is no substitute for experience. It's the one attribute that cannot be taught; it has to be acquired over time. Experience teaches us skills that can't be gained by academic study alone.

I've known Adam for a long time now, from right back when he was working for Geoff Hamilton at Barnsdale Gardens in Rutland. Geoff was a good man, a good friend and a great gardener. The fact that he took on the youngster, fresh from the Parks Department says it all: here was someone different, someone prepared to graft and learn, someone that wanted to make his way in the landscape world.

Geoff, bless him, never really trusted designers, feeling that they spent far too much of people's hard-earned cash. Having said that, he had the generosity of spirit to send Adam to study at my newly-formed design school at Capel Manor. I don't think Adam would mind me saying that he was a bit rough round the edges then, but there was no doubting his drive. Adam was going to be a designer. He was edgy to the point of being sharp and he had a good deal to learn about people skills. But those would come – it was quite obvious what he wanted to do.

Adam learned fast. One of his real strengths was his grounding in landscape construction. He was a terrific landscaper and this is really how we got to know one another. I have no idea how many gardens Adam Frost Landscapes built for me, but there were a lot. The relationship between designer and landscaper is based on trust. I've always known what I've wanted out of a scheme and Adam delivered the goods every single time – even when I got the survey wrong, which is something I'm not allowed to forget!

I've had my fair share of success at the Chelsea Flower Show and in 2005 I was working with Sir Terence Conran to create a 'Peace Garden' for the Imperial War Museum. I was responsible for the construction and planting and as far as I was concerned, there was only one person I could trust with that. Needless to say, Adam and his team produced an immaculate result. But far more important was his reaction to Terence. In my mind, this was when all of Adam's ambitions crystallised. Conran, unlike many of today's designers, came up the hard way: starting with an understanding of materials and construction, moving into design and culminating in retail. From that moment, Adam could clearly see where his road was going. Chelsea is not only a great publicity opportunity for any designer it is also a test-bed for new ideas and Adam took to it with a vengeance. Although, if he had not taken this route I'm sure he could have become an equally talented chef or footballer.

To my mind, an increasing number of Chelsea and other show gardens are clever but fail to relate to real people and real gardeners. Fashion is a dangerous companion and there is too much of it on the Chelsea catwalk. So to see a composition that works in both aesthetic and practical terms

is a breath of fresh air. It's no wonder, therefore, that Adam now has seven gold medals under his belt with, no doubt, a good few more to come.

Something that has always interested me is just where a designer gets his or her ideas from. Adam and his work have always had both a sense of place and been deeply influenced by his journey through life. All of this is reflected in his passion for gardens as a practical art form. The gardens and construction details in this book are ideas you can take home. These are ideas that are actually attainable, sustainable and for the whole

From left: Adam; HRH Princess Anne; Sir Terence Conran and David Stevens

family. In essence, they sum up his philosophy: gardens are for people and, like each and every one of us, they are unique.

Any book should of course be more than just a good read. And a work that is concerned with design should be both inspirational and full of sense – just like this one. Well done lad, you are flying.

Welcome

Over the years, I have been asked so many times, 'where do you find your inspiration year on year?', to which I normally say 'all around me – you just have to look', and leave it at that.

But, thinking back, I wanted all of these gardens to contain a little bit of me and my passion for the open countryside, architecture, art, people and food.

I never wanted to be someone I'm not. When these gardens were created I had to feel comfortable in them.

Pretentious design has never interested me. I want places to feel obtainable, comfortable but still beautiful. I have been lucky over the years to have worked with some incredible people, who have been inspirational. Writing this book has made me realise what horticulture has given me.

My professional life began with working for the North Devon Parks Department, during which time I fell in love with the North Devon landscape. Next was London, to become a landscaper, but my lucky break was getting a job with the late Geoff Hamilton at Barnsdale Gardens. This man just fuelled in me a fire to learn.

Working at Barnsdale was a dream for me, not that I probably realised it at the time. But it was with Geoff that I really started to understand what gardens could do for people. He just had a unique way of communicating and enthusing, though in a straightforward manner. It was Geoff that gave

must have been proud – as he did go on about it! So, even as a child, this place was important to me. Then, fast-forward a few years to when I was working with Geoff and we were lucky enough to get Press day tickets. I can remember feeling very privileged and it blew me away – maybe it was destiny. My first real taste of being part of Chelsea was shortly after starting my own landscape company. I was lucky enough to be involved in building various show gardens, which taught me a lot. I loved it, but it never quite felt enough. I needed to create my own Chelsea garden.

If I'm honest, when I first started designing at Chelsea I did not always feel that comfortable within the environment. But the show helped me to develop not only as a designer but also as a person, which, looking back, seems quite funny as I am now an RHS Ambassador for Secondary Education. What I love about show gardens is they give me the opportunity to explore and really get under the skin of the subject, from working on a blank sheet of paper to a finished garden. When you think about it, a show garden is probably the only time you ever finish a garden and then watch it change, even if it's only for a week. For me, understanding design is all about keeping your eyes and mind open and looking at what I call the 'second layer of life' – the detail. Everywhere I go, I try to engage with my surroundings.

I hope you take something from my ramblings, my thoughts and where I gained my inspiration as I take you on the journey of my seven Gold Medal gardens.

Every single one of these designs is special to me, and has left me with a lifetime of memories, most of them being good. Many of us make excuses that we do not have the time to garden. I believe we should all find the time as we all have the ability to create somewhere special. It does not have to be a show garden, just somewhere you can enjoy with your partner, kids, friends or family. Gardens can be such special places; they feed the soul. Hope you enjoy.

me the chance to train in garden design and he couldn't have found anybody better for me: that person was David Stevens. Where Geoff had talked of plants and how to garden, David talked of space, form and function and I loved it!

The Chelsea Flower Show was for me the Holy Grail. Chelsea seemed to have been part of my vocabulary from early years; the family stories of my first visit when I was only two to working at the show with my old man when I was 12. I can still picture myself helping on the garden with a marquee behind and the guy ropes. When on the showground, I have often wondered which site that garden was built on all those years ago. My old man worked for Gavin Jones Landscapes, who built John Brookes' early Chelsea Gardens, of which he

Thank you

John Lennon put it so well: 'You may say I'm a dreamer, but I'm not the only one'

I think we all have dreams, and I chased this one for a long time. It would not have been possible without a little help from a lot of people over many years. I have been lucky enough to have worked with some wonderful people.

I suppose I should start with the fellas that have been on most of the journey with me, Uncle Greg, Dave Harrison, Jim Buttress and of course Tats! You guys really have left me with so many memories – even though some of them I would rather forget! I wouldn't be where I am today without your help and patience.

Thanks to David Stevens, not only for the kind words in this book, but also for the years of support.

None of the gardens would have been built without teams of craftspeople/landscapers/carpenters/gardeners/growers/suppliers with one thing in common; a passion for what they do! And of course the Royal Horticulture Society for all they do.

Over the last few years I have been working for Homebase with a group of people that have been top-drawer. Developing the academy is probably the most satisfying thing I've done in my career. So a big thank you to you all.

Tats (again), Marianne Majerus, Bennet Smith and Charlie Hopper. I love the way you all capture special moments in time. Thank you for the photos.

Mark, my publisher, for believing there was a book in me that was worth doing.

And finally, my love and thanks goes to Sulina (my wife), and the kids: Abbie-Jade, Jacob, Amber-lily and Oakley. You really are my muse. Thanks for believing. Jacob you have probably read this as many times as the editor, thanks pal. xx

If I have missed anyone then thank you to you too! xx

2007

ADAM FROST LANDSCAPES

Realistic Retreat

Category: Urban garden
Award: Gold medal

I always said that if I ever got to design my own Chelsea garden, it would be as close as I could possibly make it to a 'real' garden – not over-the-top and showy, but a space which might inspire visitors to create something similar at home. So my first garden, which I named Realistic Retreat, was conceived as a first garden for a first home; for a young couple who have a passion for gardening – a rare thing today! Realistic Retreat offers a contemporary garden for a couple living in a city. A valuable resource in a highly built-up urban environment where gardens are small and space to chill-out is at a premium. Whatever the size of your garden, it's likely you'll want it to be a mixture of the practical and the beautiful. I hoped that Realistic Retreat would fulfil each of these aims as, for me, great design is simple but beautiful.

A calm and relaxing modern space has been created by playing with different textures and colours to be enjoyed by the owners and wildlife alike

This was a garden designed to be viewed from the kitchen window first: to be enjoyed as the kettle switch is flicked first thing in the morning. As the kettle boils, or the wine is uncorked at the end of a stressful day, the garden draws you in. It is a very simple, small space based on strong, uncomplicated shapes.

It uses only two materials and works because it plays with two different levels. The central space in the garden is designed for multiple uses.

A raised bed with integrated seating is alongside a raised pool which is fed by water falling off trays cut from York stone. Water is such an essential part of any garden and in this case helps to screen out city noise, while also attracting wildlife – providing a sense of calm in a busy world. The water falls into a lower pool and works its way back across the garden.

Tatsuya Shrai

"If I got to design my own Chelsea garden it would be as close as I as could possibly make it to a 'real' garden "

The focal point of Realistic Retreat is a sculpture by Pierre Bidaud inspired by pregnancy – which was fitting as my wife Sulina was pregnant at the time.

I find commissioning or finding original work is a great way of bringing something unique to any garden. Or, alternatively, I might design something and have it made. I've always had a sense that design and craft is something important. Not exclusive, not special, just important. Certain things have always caught my eye; I love creating unusual objects from stone and timber.

Maybe some of it came from my Dad who would always be making things out of stone and timber – looking back, what he could do with his hands amazes me. As I grew up I never imagined I would follow him into landscaping – even when I got a job as an apprentice at the parks department in North Devon.

I fell in love with gardens and looking after them. I soon knew I wanted to build them too. After that I wanted to design, so I did. Looking back, horticulture has really helped me to evolve as a person. I have

The shrubs like the Salix Rosmarinifolia and Continus Coggygria 'Young Lady' create an important structure to the garden

always needed to understand something, learn it, do it, and move on to the next thing.

After North Devon I spent time landscaping in London and then I was lucky enough to work for the *Gardener's World* TV presenter, the late Geoff Hamilton, at his Barnsdale garden. This man left me with not only a passion for plants but a passion for gardening and a passion to teach and pass it on.

It was Geoff who allowed me to start designing and building gardens for magazines, books and television. Looking back it was probably the best job in the world. It was an amazing time and he showed great faith in me. At the time I took it all for granted.

You can see from Geoff's TV performances what he was like. What you saw was what you got. Geoff's sudden death in 1996 removed a major figure from my life. You don't meet many people who leave as big a mark on you as he did on me. It was Geoff who helped develop my self-belief. He was a role model and I still miss him now.

You can find his work on YouTube and it still seems surprisingly fresh and, more importantly, completely relevant. Geoff was an organic gardener – pro-biodiversity, pro-conservation and anti-chemical – at a time when this was certainly not mainstream. I'm sure he'd be so pleased that it's now become accepted.

Over the years I built many gardens with Geoff and it always amazed me when designers would turn up; I'd think 'they are actually earning a living doing this'! I really wanted to be having a go at it and so I mentioned it to Geoff. He made a few phone calls to some of the leading garden designers of the time, including John Brookes, Robin Williams Snr and David Stevens, to see

York slabs help to provide contrast and give a break from the red brick. The informal planting and overhanging foliage helps soften the edges and the wisteria looks like falling water

NATIONAL ROSE GARDEN
Designed by Michael Balston
Built by Adam Frost Landscapes

In 2006, David Stevens introduced me to the Royal National Rose Society and we built their new garden at St Albans, designed by renowned landscape architect Michael Balston. The job was landscaping on a large scale!

if they'd provide me with some training. In the end Geoff thought I would get on well with David Stevens and he was right. To this day, I don't think I have met anyone with such an understanding of space.

David and I have worked together a lot and became great friends. He's one of the most positive human beings I've ever met. He's always been there to lend me an ear – as I think Geoff would have, had he lived. I've been so lucky in my career with the people who've helped me.

But back in 1996 when Geoff died so did my job as Geoff's Landscape Manager – and I had to make a living, so started my own business. Landscaping

provided an immediate remedy, as David Stevens and others stepped up to offer me work building their gardens. I kept my hand in with design, but it was always second to the landscaping work. In retrospect, that period gave me a chance to develop and understand so much about designing and landscaping. I ended up as associate designer with David Stevens International.

I now say to my students and anyone thinking of going into garden design that understanding how gardens are put together is a must, because looking back I believe that's where my passion for detail came from. By building gardens you learn to understand how materials work together.

A profound change

In 2005 I was fortunate enough to be asked by David Stevens to build the Peace Garden at Chelsea for the Imperial War Museum – commemorating the fiftieth anniversary of the end of the Second World War. It

was designed by Habitat founder Sir Terence Conran and David looked after the planting. I spent 12 months working with this pair and learned so much from them.

But I still felt a hesitancy about going into designing full-time. I felt that socially I didn't come from the same background as many of the successful designers and that I might be a square peg in a round hole.

When I was talking with Sir Terence about this one day he said "You just remember, I started as a joiner – I made things." That remark stuck in my head. It made me think "Maybe I can do it". To this day I'm not sure if Sir Terence has any idea what a profound effect he had on my life!

Having found the confidence to launch myself as a designer and leave behind the security blanket of my landscaping business, I needed to find funding. One

Above: Lighting in the upper and lower ponds adds interest at dusk. Facing: the white flowers and foliage of the wisteria help soften the hard brickwork. In winter its stems also provide interest

"It was a brilliant challenge and gave me the opportunity to create exactly the kind of garden I wanted 🙶

of my last major jobs as a landscaper was building the National Rose Garden at St Albans. This was a big job and there had been a 12-month retention of £18,000 in case of any snags. As luck would have it, this was due in time for Chelsea 2007!

But with not even £18 in our account come the end of a month, how was I going to convince my wife to spend £18,000 on a Chelsea garden? I'm not sure she quite got it at first (and probably just wanted a nice holiday), but then she concluded that if I needed to do it then I should – she really is an amazing lady.

A big investment

Although David and Sir Terence had given me the confidence to aim high, it was Sulina's incredible support and belief in me that gave me the final impetus to follow my heart. She knew that I wouldn't be satisfied until I had tried my hand at Chelsea under my own banner. But it still felt like a huge gamble.

The limestone sculpture by Pierre Bidaud acts as a focal point amongst the cottage-style planting

I submitted my application for the Urban Garden category to the RHS for Chelsea 2007 and was pleased – and if I'm honest terrified – when it was accepted. It was a brilliant challenge and gave me the opportunity to create exactly what I wanted. I didn't want to pack it with planting to be showy or to try and impress. I wanted it to feel achievable, hence the name of Realistic Retreat.

Designing a garden, whether it's for Chelsea or anywhere else is about understanding the space you have and what you want the garden to be. Is it a thoughtful, tranquil space? Or somewhere to entertain? Or for the kids to play? Or for growing vegetables? A garden can include all of these, but knowing what's wanted is essential from day one. It's easiest to break things down into two lists, which I name Practical and Individual. When I'm working with people, it's getting to know them and how they live. I never lift a pen until I have spent time understanding all of these varied needs from my clients. For me there are four things to consider when it comes to designing gardens: people, plants, space and place.

Sometimes small gardens can be more difficult to deal with design-wise than large gardens in that we want to achieve the same in both. When you start to put your Practical and Individual lists together you can

"Focal points like a piece of sculpture draw your eye – especially in a small garden like Realistic Retreat"

Tatsuya Shrai

"It is important in any garden to consider the boundaries as part of the overall design 🙶

figure out how to fit your ideas into a small space.

Each of my Chelsea gardens is considered and researched – from the hard landscaping, sculpture, structures, ornaments through to the furniture. To ensure I'm focused I always create an imaginary client for my show gardens.

Maximising the design is about being a bit clever with levels, using retaining walls, built-in furniture, extra outdoor storage and not over-complicating the space. Taking a lead from the architecture is the key to making sure your design ties back to the house and looks like it's meant to be there.

In any garden it is important to consider boundaries as part of the design; with Realistic Retreat I envisaged working with the brick walls of a town house. Here there is a mix of traditional and contemporary, sawn York stone and red brick, with clean geometric lines.

If brickwork had been used for all the surfaces it would have looked too heavy, especially as the house walls and the walls in the garden were brick. Each

Fine-beaded detailing on the sandstone coping is picked up on the front of the wooden seat. For continuity, the sawn sandstone is also used for the paving in the background

Tatsuya Shrai

"I knew I didn't want to go back to landscaping and I was determined to be a garden designer 𝄢

of my Chelsea gardens is considered and researched – from the hard landscaping, sculpture, structures, ornaments through to the furniture.

I wanted a specific handmade look for the red-brick walls and ended up visiting a number of brick-manufacturers to find exactly the right one. I even made a few myself at the York Handmade Brick company and I loved it. It's great that we could showcase the craft of brickmaking.

We have wonderful traditional crafts in this country and it is great to be able support and celebrate them wherever we can.

I chose English Garden Bond as the pattern for our brick wall in Realistic Retreat, which gives a good contrast to the modern sawn York stone. There are many brick bonds, traditional and modern, to choose from when you are building hard structure and each one creates a different feel. You can view a few different brick bonds at the end of this chapter.

Exuberant and cottage-style planting using **Rosa 'Souvenir du Docteur Jamain', Astrantia Major 'Roma'** *and* **Persicaria bistorta 'Superba'** *against a backdrop of* **Salix Rosmarinifolia**

SCULPTURE
Pierre Bidaud

Tatsuya Shrai

I knew Pierre Bidaud through working on several landscaping projects and when I mentioned I was looking for a piece of sculpture for my Chelsea garden, he kindly lent me this beautiful piece of work. The sculpture was inspired by pregnancy, which was great as my wife was pregnant at the time and so it seemed very fitting. The white of the limestone sculpture is highlighted against a backdrop of green, with white highlights provided by the foxgloves and roses, which provides a cohesive feel with the sawn York stone paving.

Using brick on both walls and floors can bring a sense of harmony and it can provide a warmth and texture that is pleasing to the eye.

In Realistic Retreat the sawn York stone softens the effect of the brickwork and brings a different kind of reflected light to the area. We also used York stone for the water trays, the water chutes, and on the bottom of the pool. York stone is a near-perfect material. Here it looks smooth and contemporary (although it can also look rough-hewn) but it speaks of a tradition that goes back to medieval times, and the stone has been mined from quarries in Yorkshire ever since. If I'd been Dick Whittington I wouldn't have been disappointed that the streets of London weren't paved with gold; they were paved with York stone, something just as good in my eyes.

Focal points

Realistic Retreat was designed to have lots of local interest so that there is always something beautiful and interesting to draw your eye. The sculpture, the falling wisteria and the water were all employed to do this job.

From the kitchen window the owners can see the sculpture, but the water feature on the left-hand side is tucked away and it only becomes visible when you wander further down through the garden. You hear the water before you see it – creating a sense of surprise.

Although this garden is designed primarily for a couple to use I imagined they'd want to entertain and that friends and family would be using it too. I had to

The white flower of the wisteria is picked up in the magnolia: both are iconic plants and can work in smaller gardens

think about where they might sit, but traditional tables and chairs would clutter the space and potentially interfere with the flow of the garden, so I created a wall and bench. The soft planting scheme contrasts with the modernity of the house and the geometry of the garden. I used roses, geraniums, salvias, roses and foxgloves, plants that people would recognise, to achieve that cottage garden feel. The sculptural rodgersia sits in water in a pot, which means that it can be pulled out for protection in winter. The planting scheme is designed to be low maintenance.

I'm lucky in having worked with plants all my life and having a knowledge of what works in different positions. But like many designers I always like to experiment with plants. There may be a huge range in the garden centre and lots of 'experts' explaining what and what not to do. But, if I plant something and it doesn't work, or grows too big, or if I just don't like it there, it can nearly always be moved!

Trees and shrubs

When I'm planning the planting scheme for a garden I see trees and large shrubs as part of the structure of the garden – thinking of them in terms of height and spread. Although at the outset I usually don't know exactly what plants I'm going to choose I still plot shapes onto the overall design and fill in the detail later in the process.

For most of us, how we live – our colour schemes, furniture and accessories – change and evolve. So it is with gardens and what you like to put in them. A garden is a playground for experimentation and finding yourself. Learn what you like by trying plants and be prepared to change as time goes on.

On the subject of playful experimentation, I was really pleased by the choice of wisteria grown against the brick wall. The fall of the wisteria flowers echoes the falling water and is an example of how planting

Tatsuya Shrai

"Clients have told me that learning to tend their gardens has changed their lives 🥺

can be used to complement structural elements in design. I love wisteria. It is an incredible plant, with a palette that ranges from creamy white to deep purple and all the shades of lilac in between. It is a wonderful architectural climber and looks great even without its leaves.

Planting should give a good sense of the seasons. Whatever the time of year, there should be something of interest in your garden; from snowdrops in winter to the autumn colour of the field maple.

Light is another important element in a garden. Orientation will dictate where the light plays, where shadows form, where the sun rises and sets and, ultimately, where plants will grow. Light is an incredibly powerful force of nature which we take for granted, but it can be used as a tool for creating effects and illusions. Think of the atmosphere that can be created by lighting in a cleverly lit room. It's the same principle in a garden. When the sun goes down in this garden, dappled shadows are created across the reflective water, and the York stone is the perfect foil for a long evening shadow.

The water pours freely from the lower spout creating an image of power and drama, but only trickles from the top spout to the one below making a gentler sound and creating a softer image

"Once you're hooked on gardening you'll feel deprived if you can't get into your garden 〞

Gardening is an elemental thing. Once you're hooked you'll feel deprived if you can't get into your garden. Clients tell me that learning to tend and nurture their gardens has changed their life.

Being judged

But back at the show, how would the judges view my first Chelsea offering? More importantly, what would the visiting public think? Ultimately, I care more about what the general public think than the judges – though of course it's great to win a Gold Medal and it does mean a lot professionally.

I had no expectations at all about the outcome – I just wanted to build a garden exactly how I had imagined it and be pleased with the result.

Although the Gold Medal was brilliant, a big moment for me was seeing my old man visit the garden. He'd recently suffered a stroke and was in a wheelchair. When he arrived and stood up to admire my garden it

Light and shade add so much to a garden. The shadow cast by the wall was very much in contrast to the hot feeling of the sunny side

meant a lot more to me than I would have imagined. Not that he said a lot, just nodded.

When I think about this time I can see how I've developed as a designer. After my first Chelsea success with Realistic Retreat I knew that I was never going to look back, and I never have. It's certainly not an easy way to make a living but I love my work and that's a great thing to be able to say. I couldn't have done it without the support of people around me.

I've discovered, through my journey, that if you can follow your heart then you should do so. Be creative! You won't regret it.

Details, like continuing the bead from the limestone across the front of the seat, are small things but they make a big difference

Tatsuya Shrai

Tatsuya Shrai

Wisteria sinensis 'Alba'

My favourite climber, a wonderful plant with lovely white hanging, pea-like flowers in spring and early summer. Will grow to heights of 20m and enjoys sheltered conditions

Astrantia major 'Roma'

A great worker that will grow up to 0.75m. The paper-like flowers are deep pink and will flower from early summer and can carry on all the way through

Rosa Paul's Himalayan Musk

A cracking rambler, which is also a profuse flowerer. Has white flowers that will grow in clusters. This plant will grow up to 10m. It also has a musky fragrance

Rosa 'Souvenir du Docteur Jamain'

I love the fact that this rose grows happily in shady conditions. It will grow up to 1.7m if left. However it can be controlled. The deep claret flowers have a great scent and will flower throughout the summer if clean-headed

Salix Rosmarinifolia

A great willow that I love. They have fine leaves that look like Rosemary, hence the name. The dark brown stalks bear long leaves that turn a dark yellow in autumn. The plant is able to grow up to 4m in well-drained soil with exposure to the sun

Persicaria bistorta superba

An useful plant that sits happily in both cottage and native type plantings. It has a lovely pink bottle-brush like flower that sits above a dock-like leaf. It favours being exposed to the sun and in soil that isn't too moist

Rodgersia pinnata

A moisture-loving bushy plant that has green foliage all year round. This plant blossoms in summer and grows sprays of fluffy pink and cream flowers. It enjoys being sheltered from the sun and is able to grow between 1m-1.5m tall

Cotinus coggygria 'Young Lady'

A small shrub that grows between 1m-1.5m in well-drained soil and exposure to the sun. It has delicate oval-shaped leaves, wonderful cloud-like flowers and a good autumn colour

Garden layout

This garden is very simple in shape, providing a good, usable space that is brought alive with the planting. This provides interest and a cottage-garden style. A lot of effort was put into material choice: York handmade bricks with sawn York stone — a classic combination.

What I call the 'second layer' of this garden was also important. The stone coping bead detail is carried through the end of the timber seat – which projects over the brick retaining wall. Using a focal point sculpture is a great way of putting your mark on a space. The focal point captures your attention and draws you in.

I love using water as a surface, it plays with the light and encourages wildlife. Sitting the water tray on the left-hand side not only provides sound but adds interest as you move down into the garden.

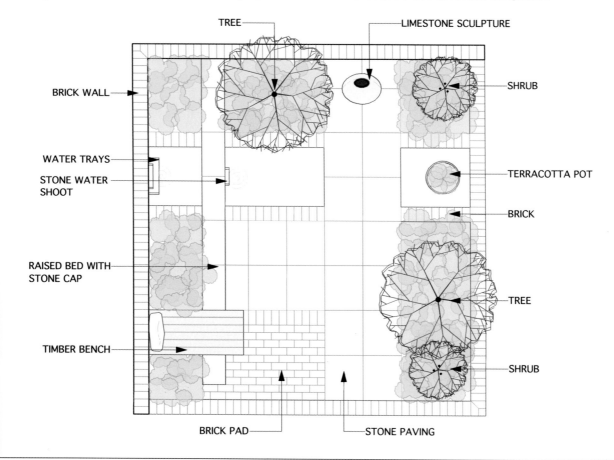

TREE

LIMESTONE SCULPTURE

BRICK WALL

SHRUB

WATER TRAYS

STONE WATER SHOOT

TERRACOTTA POT

BRICK

RAISED BED WITH STONE CAP

TREE

TIMBER BENCH

SHRUB

BRICK PAD

STONE PAVING

Brick bonds I

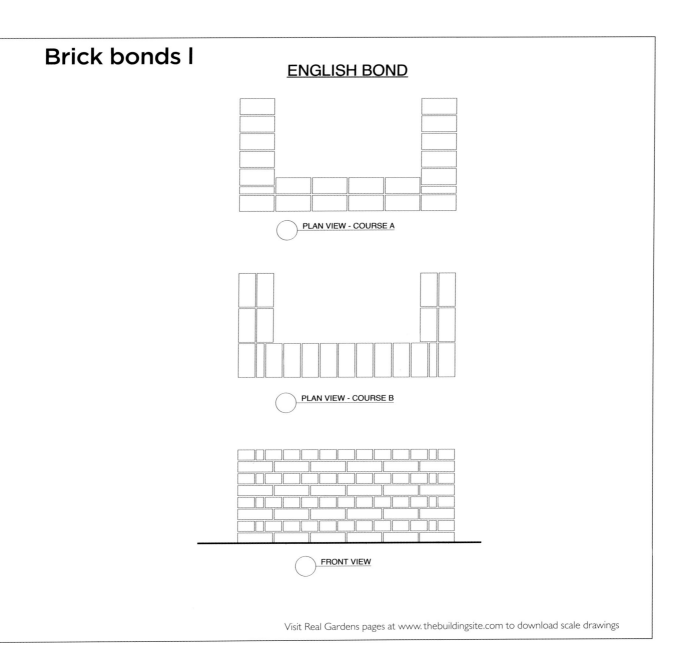

ENGLISH BOND

PLAN VIEW - COURSE A

PLAN VIEW - COURSE B

FRONT VIEW

Visit Real Gardens pages at www.thebuildingsite.com to download scale drawings

Brick bonds II

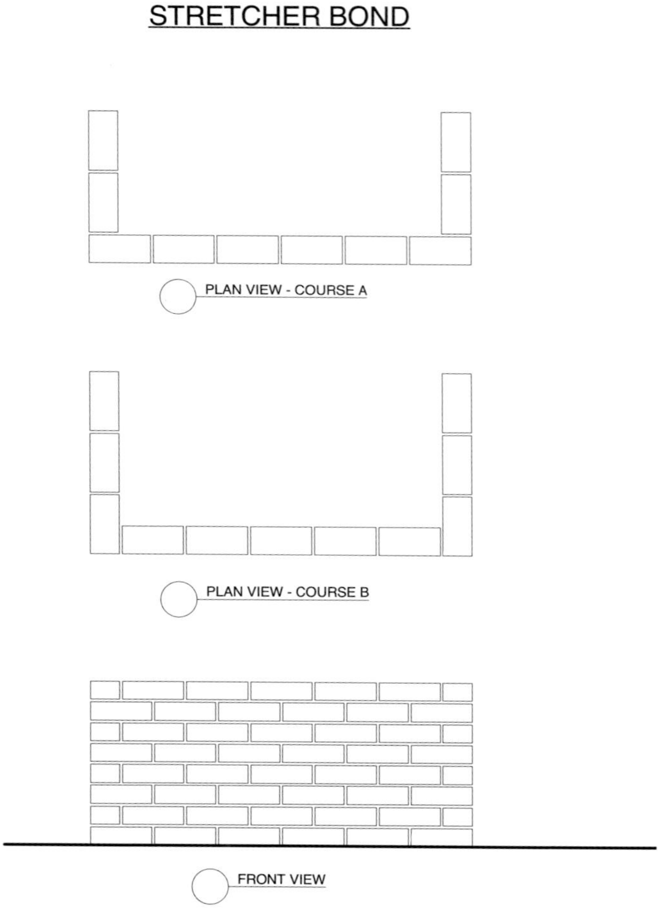

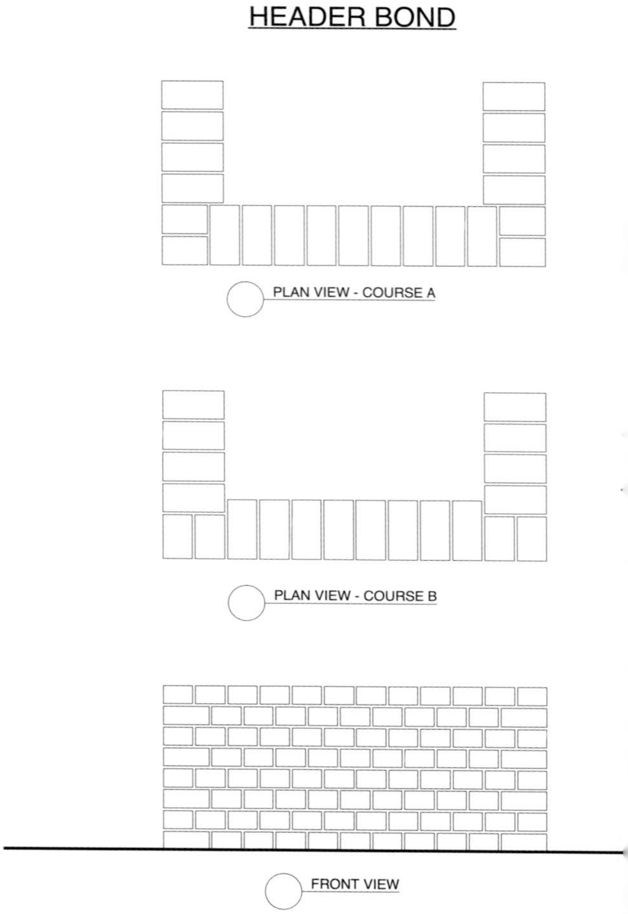

STRETCHER BOND

PLAN VIEW - COURSE A

PLAN VIEW - COURSE B

FRONT VIEW

HEADER BOND

PLAN VIEW - COURSE A

PLAN VIEW - COURSE B

FRONT VIEW

Brick bonds III

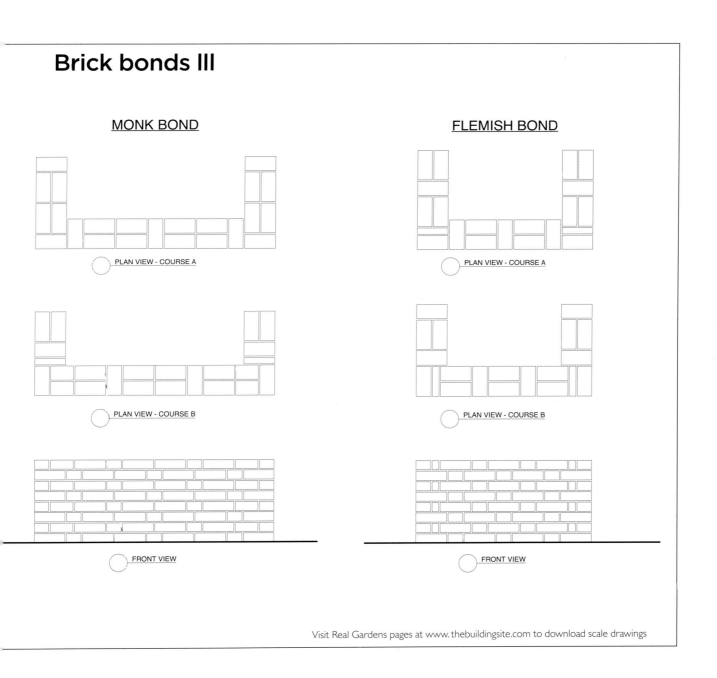

MONK BOND

PLAN VIEW - COURSE A

PLAN VIEW - COURSE B

FRONT VIEW

FLEMISH BOND

PLAN VIEW - COURSE A

PLAN VIEW - COURSE B

FRONT VIEW

Visit Real Gardens pages at www.thebuildingsite.com to download scale drawings

Water feature

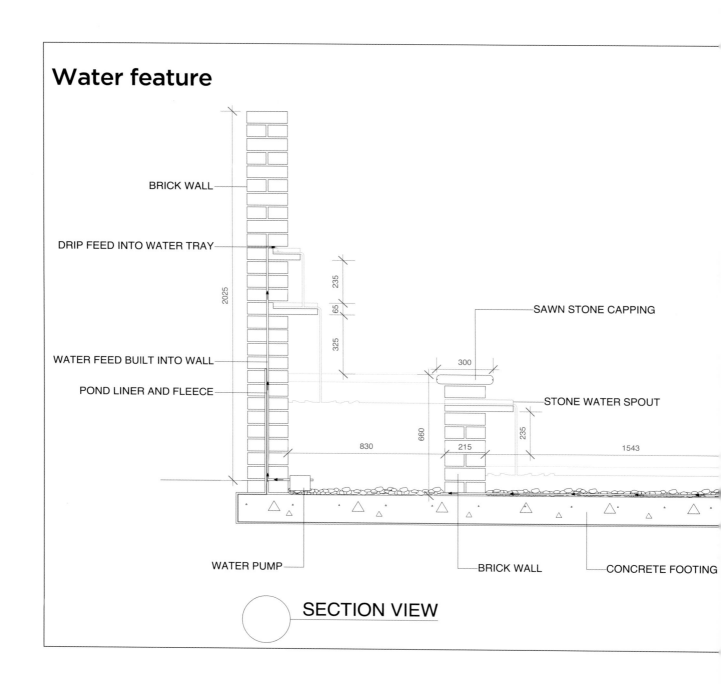

BRICK WALL

DRIP FEED INTO WATER TRAY

235

65

325

2025

SAWN STONE CAPPING

WATER FEED BUILT INTO WALL

POND LINER AND FLEECE

300

STONE WATER SPOUT

660

235

830

215

1543

WATER PUMP

BRICK WALL

CONCRETE FOOTING

SECTION VIEW

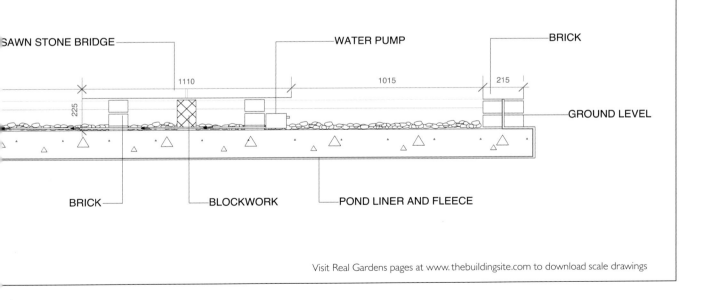

SAWN STONE BRIDGE ————————————————— WATER PUMP ————— BRICK

1110   1015   215

225

GROUND LEVEL

BRICK ————— BLOCKWORK ————— POND LINER AND FLEECE

Visit Real Gardens pages at www.thebuildingsite.com to download scale drawings

2008

ADAM FROST LANDSCAPES

A Welcome Sight

Category: Urban garden
Award: Gold medal/Best in Show

I remember vividly a time when my grandmother and her friends would stand in their front gardens chatting with each other and with anyone who happened to be passing. Their front gardens were a sociable space and something to be proud of. Nowadays, people are paving over their gardens to make spaces for ever more cars. What would you rather see from your front window: the bonnet of a car or a green space?

With this in mind, for Chelsea 2008 I designed A Welcome Sight and, as before, I created an imaginary client. This time it was an urban couple living in a small townhouse who wanted to maintain a beautiful green space at the front of their house. Like many front gardens, it was only a small area and, like all small spaces, every little part needed thinking through.

Small areas are often more difficult than larger ones. The whole of a small space is visible in one go and there isn't the option of moving from one space to another. I like crafted detail – something that makes the space yours. I wanted this couple to walk to their front door through an inviting green room.

Front gardens with trees, shrubs, grass, water and perennials are a welcome sight not only for the home owners but for anyone passing by. I care passionately about the loss of our front gardens and the impact on wildlife. We just destroy habitats without a second thought.

A steel rill carries water from beside the front door through the planting and into a lower pool

"The layout of this garden is inspired by the old tenet that 'an Englishman's home is his castle' "

Aside from the community aspect of the garden, I wanted to create a place that the owners would be proud of, where they could sit for a while after the stresses and strains of the working day. So the layout of this garden is inspired by the old tenet that 'an Englishman's home is his castle'. With this in mind, I created a moat waterway which the owners would have to cross before they reached the sanctuary of their front door. The water runs widthways across the garden and the coursed brick path that leads up to the front door gives the impression of a drawbridge. I wanted to create the feeling that once they reached the wide steps at the front they were on home ground.

A very important feature of this garden is water and, whether the garden is viewed from the street or from the house, I wanted the owners to see the water. Two steel rills sit over the pool; the one on the left-hand side draws you into the garden and the one on the right leads you out of the garden.

Water is a surface, used here to complement and

The steel rill gives the illusion of being held up by the Buxus hedging. In reality a steel post, screened by the planting, did the job

*Clouds of **Alchemilla mollis** add a fresh lime colour to the garden*

contrast with the other surfaces. Water also makes a space seem bigger and the reflection of the sky brings that vast expanse into the garden. It creates a whole new source of light. There should be nothing heavy or dark in a front garden; it should be open and dappled, not uninterrupted blocks of stone or colour. A Welcome Sight has the light and airy feel of a spring morning.

Another important detail of this garden is the wide steps, which run the width of the garden. They are deliberately out of proportion with the small space, and the door is not set in the middle of the steps as you would normally expect. Having wider steps makes the whole garden feel wider than it is and they also make a great place to sit. If we had used narrow ones directly in front of the door, we would have created a void on either side, an area we could have filled with plants, but by using the lovely light Derbyshire sandstone

The brick path across the water creates the feeling of a drawbridge over a moat

*The terracotta tones of
handmade herb pots tie in with
the red brick path*

steps we created an interesting, dynamic space. The walls on either side of the drawbridge and in front of the steps also provide a sense of enclosure.

The arbour over the front door houses small hidden pipes which allow water to gently run down over the corkscrew sculptures into the pool below. The water in the pool flows along the rill and then falls back into the moat to be pumped up again. The rills themselves are made from steel, sprayed a gunmetal colour, which gives a contemporary feel and contrasts beautifully with the white-rendered walls. The colour of the steel rills also harmonises with the *Prunus serrula* just behind. The rendered walls and light sandstone paving help make the area feel brighter. In the afternoon the sun shone through the trees creating interesting shadows in the rills and pools. More interest was created by the water that dripped from the sculpture – creating hypnotic rings that moved to the edge of the small pool.

The large corkscrew sculptures by the front door hint at the bottle of wine waiting for the couple at the

DESIGNING FOR PLACE
Keeping in harmony with your surroundings

When I start to design any garden, the first question I always ask is does the garden sit comfortably within its own environs? Is there harmony between the garden and the house? Just as importantly, particularly in the case of A Welcome Sight, is there harmony between the garden and the rest of the street? A beautiful space full of wonderful plants and a place to sit and pass the time of day has, in my opinion, to fit that bill. But when you are designing a front garden, it is definitely the time to be sympathetic to the surrounding area, as well as your neighbours. You can't simply impose a modern contemporary structure amidst a row of cottage gardens. There ought to be a connection between the space, the building and the streetscape. That's not to say there can't be contemporary elements in any garden, but think and plan so that the space you create adds to the general environment and doesn't stick out like a sore thumb.

If you want to design a front garden that is bold and welcoming, my advice would be to pay attention to your surroundings: to the general tone of the area; to the type of architecture of your own house and those around; to what is often termed the local 'vernacular'. Look past the 'first layer' of what you see and drill down into the detail of what surrounds you, in terms of structure and colour. Are there tiny aspects of your own house, or others, that you can replicate, such as architectural features like stone lintels or porch supports? Are there colours which you can pick up and echo in your planting scheme? You don't have to imitate any of these details overtly but you can reference them in a subtle way.

For example, in A Welcome Sight, the warm

red of the brickwork is echoed in the *Prunus serrula* stems and is carried on through the planting with *Heuchera 'Brownies'* and *Anthriscus 'Ravenswing'*. Because the house is modern in style, I have used architectural plants such as the acer, buxus and grasses. These not only add shape and texture but help to create a light, modern feel to the garden. The fresh lime green of the foliage is carried through the planting scheme, adding a sense of freshness to a very urban space.

These days, people think nothing of living in streets where they not only don't speak to their neighbours, they often don't even know who they are; something that would have been unheard of just a generation ago. I am deeply concerned and feel sad that we are losing our vital sense of community. Can this be right?

With A Welcome Sight, I wanted to create a garden that should connect us with nature and with each other again. As human beings, our desire for socialising and companionship is hard-wired into us and should be recognised.

"I jumped up and down like an excited kid when we unwrapped the corkscrew sculptures "

end of a long day! The corkscrews hang from the oak arbour, which in turn takes its reference from the oak on the facade of the house and from the oak front door. I designed the corkscrews and had them made by Tim Mackereth and his team at Anwick Forge. I saw the corkscrews for the very first time on site at Chelsea, and I can say with all honesty that I jumped up and down like an excited kid when we unwrapped them. They were spot-on and far exceeded my expectations.

Anwick Forge is a small business based near Sleaford, Lincolnshire, and its craftsmen are part of the army of unsung heroes who helped me realise the detail of my gardens. Tim, his wife Fran and the team at Anwick have worked with me on most of my Chelsea gardens and without them the gardens would have been missing some of the unique and deeply satisfying elements that make them special.

One of the visitors to Chelsea in 2008 was His Royal Highness, Prince Philip, and he loved the corkscrews and what they symbolised. We both agreed that the rills should have been running with red wine, not water – but we weren't sure that the RHS would approve!

The garden was designed to draw you into the space whilst adding to the streetscape

The steel corkscrews work as a focal point and draw you in, but you only notice there is water running down the corkscrews (creating rings in the pool below) as you arrive at the front door. These add a unique feature to the space.

"This garden plays with levels and materials to create added interest in a small space 🔊

I love introducing different levels into a small space. Levels transform a garden into a journey, from the roof of an arbour to the depth of a rill or pool. The final level or layer in any garden is created by the differing heights of the trees, shrubs and plants within it.

This garden plays with levels to create added interest in a small area. The raised bed on the left of the garden doubles as a seat, with oak replacing the sawn stone coping for comfort and style. Overhead, the palmate leaves of the acer form a canopy under which the owners can sit, feeling less on show, and enjoy the sound of running water.

The path from the front entrance draws you into the space and the static pattern of the paving is designed to make you pause and look around. I used 50mm bricks from Vande Moortel, a Belgian brick company, for the 'drawbridge' area. The bricks are narrower than their English counterparts, so they have a lighter feel to them.

The Vande Moortel brickwork is also used for the

In the pond at the far end of the rill can be seen the drips from the sculpture hitting the surface of the water

"I produce planting plans, but I still like to set the plants myself and place them so that they feel right 🙶

wall on the left, creating a contrast with the smooth sandstone.

The rendered walls that support the steel rills on either side of the garden tie back to the rendered walls of the house, giving an overall sense of cohesion and harmony.

Two intertwined forged 'vines' formed the vertical support for the oak arbour. Handmade terracotta pots from Wichford pottery contain an assortment of herbs and are placed around the garden. The owners can pick these herbs for their evening meal or just release the scent by touching them as they sit on the steps or on the walls beside the rills.

The hard landscaping – walls, paving, arbours, rills etc – is one half of a successful garden design; the other is the planting. It's the most personal part and

Buxus cubes create the illusion of supporting the steel rills with water flowing between the irises

Shadows play across the garden showing how the garden changes throughout the day as the light changes and moves around

that's why we all create different gardens – even from the same plants.

When I'm designing a garden I treat the major shrubs and trees as part of the structure – they are put on the plan in the same way as an arbour or wall. When I add them I may not know what variety they'll be, I'll just have an idea of size and shape in my head. They are part of the bones of the garden.

Each Chelsea I build up a list of plants that I want to use for the show garden. This will contain plants of the colour, shape, size and texture I need. The list gets sent to the growers and then the waiting game begins. No two growing seasons are ever the same and even during the show build-up I'll be getting news that a

plant may have peaked too early or may not be ready in time. That is part of the thrill. And besides, sometimes a last-minute replacement turns out better than the original choice.

Show planting depends on an understanding of shape, form, habitat and texture – but also teaches you about these things. In effect, you are trying to order nature. The trick is putting plants together that look

Water cascading down into the pool creates interest and sound – useful in an urban environment as it helps to mask road and other noise and is also great for wildlife

like they belong and that they've always been there. That's why I look for the patterns in nature and how they repeat.

I build up the show garden in layers, with some of the larger herbaceous plants going in first. But in this garden I then put in an achimilla, and as I knew it had to repeat somewhere in the garden, I went and stood another achimilla in the general area I thought it would go. The iris behind the achimilla (by the taxus

Using the acer near the front of the garden creates screening, ensuring not all of the garden is in view all the time

Rich-coloured Belgian bricks were used for the path over the water, creating the feeling of a drawbridge over a moat

on the left-hand side) was a key plant in that it was a strong vertical against the horizontal of the water.

A lot of the planting is about a feeling and that is something that's hard to teach. It's like learning a musical instrument. We can all get pleasure from learning to play, but some can take it further. Similarly, everyone can plant a garden and get great pleasure from it – but planting a successful show garden is a lot tougher.

So, at Chelsea, I know my general structure of plants

"Colours in the garden move from dark crimson through to pinks and blues 🎏

before I start building – but exactly how they are used is one of the last things that gets decided.

In this garden, even though they are not big, the buxus cubes were architectural and I deliberately placed some to look like part of the infrastructure – as though they were holding up the steel rills. More buxus cubes work through the planting, down to the front of the garden. The *Prunus serrula* either side of the garden is a wonderful multi-stemmed tree with a deep cherry colour all year round, and bark that peels off in strips. In this garden it provides both interest and screening. It is also extremely tactile and it's hard to resist helping the bark peel off or enjoying the smoothness of the new bark beneath.

The strong structure of the trees and shrubs was softened by using *Iris sibirica*, *Stipia arundinacea* and *Stipia gigantia* throughout the garden. I added the fresh green of buxus and acers. Touches of richness were provided by astrantia, heuchera and aquilegia, picking up on the rich, red hue of the *Prunus serrula*.

More strong verticals were provided by verbascums and digitalis. The colours in the garden moved from dark crimson through to pinks and blues, finishing with the fresh lime of

Water is an important element and creates an interesting surface in a garden. The constant movement adds an ever-changing element

Alchemilla mollis. In the foreground I planted *Iris siberica*, with its rich, bright-blue flowers. Persicaria adds pops of pale pink.

As always, my aim was to create a real garden, one that could work and make people stop and think about what could be done with an outdoor space – one that would be great for the neighbourhood. It certainly went down well and won not only gold but also Best In Show in the Urban Garden category. If winning a first gold medal is daunting, the second is always harder! We were really up against it that year as we were also building a large show garden for designer Clare Agnew, who won silver-gilt.

The conversation about front gardens is still ongoing and we are not much nearer to encouraging people to fill them with plants not cars. The RHS has only now released 'About Front Gardens' 10 years on from when I created this garden.

"The garden won not only Gold but also Best in Show in the Urban Garden category 𝟻𝟻

Today, one in four UK front gardens is completely paved over and nearly one in three front gardens has no plants. I believe it is vital to reverse this trend: for the nation's health; for the good of wildlife; to mitigate against pollution and heat waves; and to help protect the UK's homes from flooding. I, for one, will be doing all I can to encourage people to green up their front gardens. Will you join me?

Iris sibirica 'Tropic night'

I love sibirica-type irises and 'Tropic night' has velvety violet flowers with beautiful yellow shoots. It is happy in sun and partial shade and grows in any good garden soil. It will grow to about 1.5m tall

Acer palamatum

The Japanese maple is most happy in a sheltered position. In time it will grow up to 8m tall and its palm-shaped leaves have a fantastic autumn colour

Anemanthele lessoniana

This evergreen perennial grass is a valuable plant; its narrow green arching leaves turn a wonderful orange-red colour as the summer moves on. From midsummer it carries a mass of rosy flowers. As it matures, it will grow up to 0.9m

Buxus sempervirens

Common box is great for bringing a sense of formality and architecture to any garden. Can be used in many ways, this evergreen shrub is a good foil for herbaceous plants

Heuchera 'Brownies'

A robust heuchera with architectural leaves which are a chocolatey brown colour. It will grow in sun or partial shade; happy in a rich, moist, retentive soil

Alchemilla mollis

A really good working plant which will self-seed if left, something I love. If you're not sure you want lots more plants then trim flowers back before they seed. The plant delivers a mass of small yellow flowers

Aquilegia vulgaris 'Ruby Port'

A great old-fashioned plant known as 'Granny's Bonnet', it has ferny green leaves and carries deep red flowers with a lovely eye. Grows happily in most soils. It is short-lived but self-seeds; great used with grasses

Stipa gigantea

The evergreen grass has wonderful golden oat-like flowers which are on stems of up to 2m tall. Grows well in a sunny position and brings a great sense of movement to any space

Garden layout

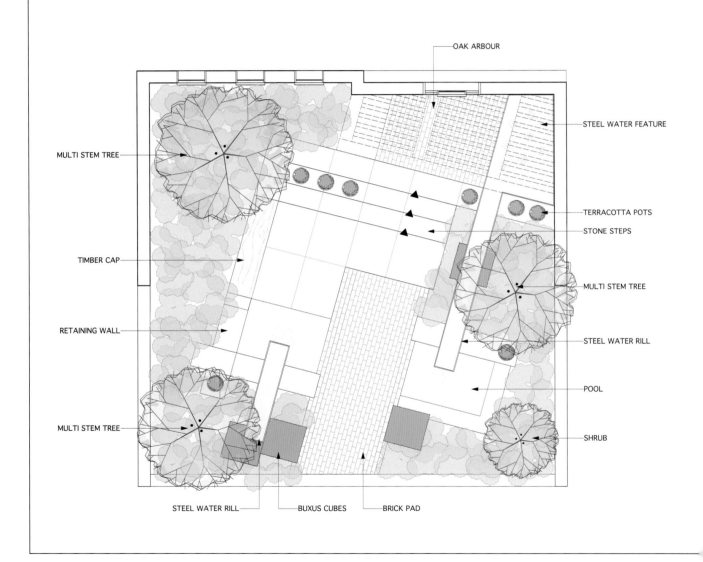

OAK ARBOUR

STEEL WATER FEATURE

MULTI STEM TREE

TERRACOTTA POTS

STONE STEPS

TIMBER CAP

MULTI STEM TREE

STEEL WATER RILL

RETAINING WALL

POOL

MULTI STEM TREE

SHRUB

STEEL WATER RILL

BUXUS CUBES

BRICK PAD

Front gardens are a big passion of mine. I feel that this urban garden doesn't just provide for the resident but the street too, because the design works on both fronts. The water and the front design work as a moat and catch your eye, with the bridge pulling you into the space.

The steel rills flow in and out of the garden so it works as you move in and when you leave the space. The wider steps are very welcoming but can also provide extra seating.

Small spaces benefit from a change of levels by providing more interest. Designing on an angle can give more movement; keeping the central area clear provides a place to pause and enjoy the space.

The materials were chosen to reflect the architecture of the house, with the bricks used for the bridge also being used in the lower walls – all great materials in an urban environment.

Wide steps

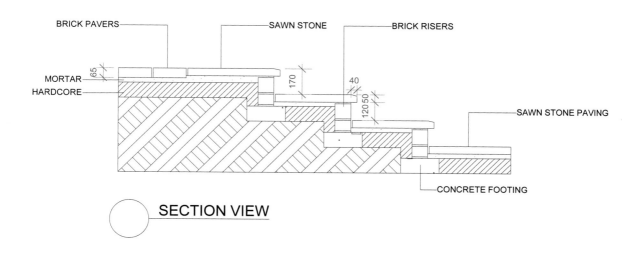

BRICK PAVERS — SAWN STONE — BRICK RISERS

MORTAR
HARDCORE

65

170

40

12050

SAWN STONE PAVING

CONCRETE FOOTING

SECTION VIEW

Visit Real Gardens pages at www.thebuildingsite.com to download scale drawings

Water feature

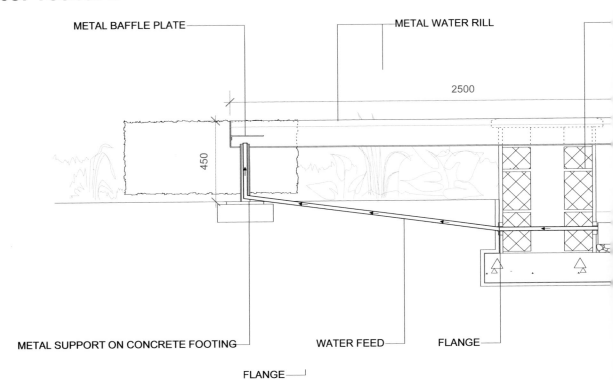

METAL BAFFLE PLATE

METAL WATER RILL

2500

450

METAL SUPPORT ON CONCRETE FOOTING

WATER FEED

FLANGE

FLANGE

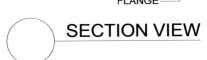

SECTION VIEW

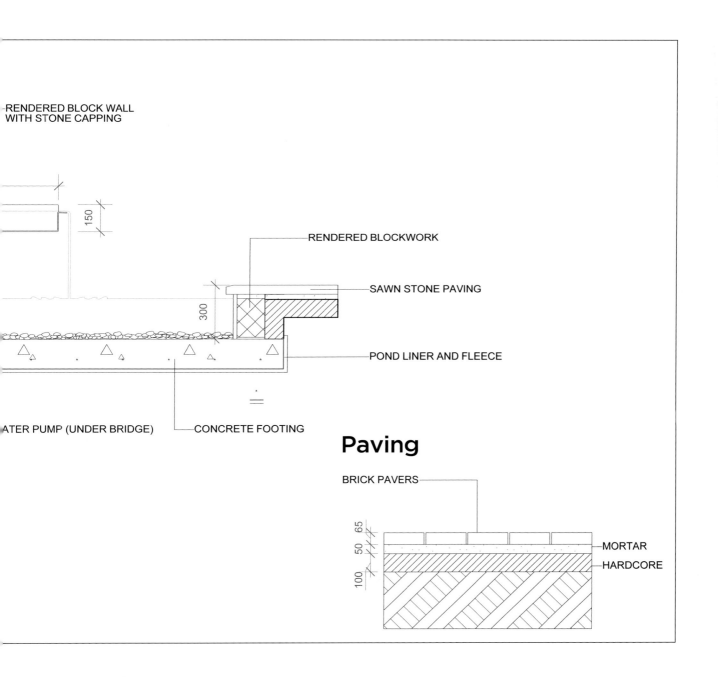

RENDERED BLOCK WALL
WITH STONE CAPPING

150

RENDERED BLOCKWORK

SAWN STONE PAVING

300

POND LINER AND FLEECE

ATER PUMP (UNDER BRIDGE)   CONCRETE FOOTING

Paving

BRICK PAVERS

65
50
100

MORTAR
HARDCORE

2011

SPONSOR: LAND'S END

Across the Pond

Category: Urban garden
Award: Gold medal

My 2011 Chelsea garden, Across the Pond, was inspired by the great American architect and designer, Frank Lloyd Wright – who was a fascinating character and a hero of mine. He once described himself as the greatest architect in the world and I'm not sure I'd disagree with that. This man's talent encompassed absolutely every aspect of design and his buildings have stood the test of time, still looking modern today. Across the Pond draws on Wright's seamless blending of nature and the built environment. It features two of his favourite materials, concrete and steel, blended with a calm planting palette. Its biggest inspiration is probably

The gap between the stepping stones is oversize to slow you down and therefore make you more aware of your surroundings

his most famous building: Fallingwater.

Creating the garden was a joy because it allowed me the chance to study him and his work in detail. As I worked out at the gym, I listened to interviews with Wright on my iPod. In them, he talked about everything from life to design; at times sounding arrogant and also incredibly charming. The more I learned about Wright,

The Shady conditions are the perfect environment for hostas and ferns

Buxus tables alongside the slabs of concrete provide another dimension

the more his vision inspired me. He was a strong advocate of organic architecture and blending the built environment with nature. He once said that nature was his church, an idea I love.

Wright pushed boundaries in every way. And his staff were amazed that, nine months into being commissioned to design Fallingwater, there was nothing on paper. So when the staff heard that Edgar Kauffmann, who had

"When designing the garden I took to heart Frank Lloyd Wright's tenet that form must follow function 🙶

commissioned Wright, was paying a surprise visit to check on progress, they feared the worst. But Wright sat down after receiving the news and proceeded to draw the house in astonishing detail. Kauffmann had no idea when he arrived that he was looking at two hours work! But in a way he wasn't. The gestation had taken all of the nine months, it's just that it was in Wright's imagination. Design does take time to develop. Sometimes, the concept comes quite quickly, but it's the detail that takes the time to perfect.

I knew from the outset that I wanted to design a garden that took its inspiration from Fallingwater, in terms of layout, materials and concept. I took to heart Wright's tenet that 'form must follow function' and created a space which was designed to provide a sanctuary for a young city couple with a modern house, possibly with concrete worktops, floors etc who wanted a garden to sit with the house. A garden featuring polished concrete and steel. I imagined the garden as somewhere they could walk into on a Sunday morning with rolled-up jeans and bare feet to read the papers.

It was a calm, relaxing place for them to escape the

A simple series of polished concrete slabs pulls you through the space to Wright-inspired seating

"It gave me the feeling you could sit there and dangle your feet in the water – as if you could touch nature 🙶

hustle and bustle of the city. As it was a city garden, everything had to fit into a small area.

The overall structure is inspired by the ingenious feat of engineering at Fallingwater, where the waterfall emerges from under the building. Cantilevered concrete creates a feeling that the house is an extension of the rock face and I wanted to try and distill this feeling. We started with the concrete water wall, which echoes the waterfall, and had this falling into the L-shaped pool, while slabs provided pathways and seating areas. At Fallingwater, under the cantilevered floors above, there is a flight of stairs leading down to a concrete pad that appears to float, unsupported, above the water. It gave me the feeling that you could sit there and dangle one's feet in the water – as if you could touch nature.

In this garden, concrete slabs sit over the L-shaped canal, creating a place to bring cushions, lie down and contemplate the sky – or to dangle ones feet in the water.

This garden was my homage to Frank Lloyd Wright and Fallingwater in particular. In my version, the form of the house is compressed into the layers of concrete

Texture and form are created by Dryopteris, Carex and Rodgersia whilst Digitalis, Luzula and Astrantia provide soft colour

"For me, there is nothing purer than the combination of woodland and water that surrounds Fallingwater 🙶

slabs that take you up and down through the garden.

The effect of these subtle changes of level is to create a sense of space and movement – making the garden feel much larger than its small urban-sized plot. The effect is to intentionally slow you down as you walk through the garden, allowing you the time and opportunity to take in your surroundings.

The slabs themselves are in fact concrete poured into metal trays. We polished them on site, which made us rather unpopular with our Chelsea garden neighbours because of the amount of dust we created. These trays of concrete created strong, simple shapes which are very beautiful and an effective detail in an urban garden. We chose to polish the concrete, rather than leaving it raw as Wright did, because I like the way polished concrete is often used in commercial

The modular seating is designed to be functional – but also interesting by being triangular in plan

The pebbles are an attractive feature, with the edge planting of Alchemilla mollis and Hostas reflecting in the water

Aesculus, digitalis and dryopteris reflect beautifully on the concrete wall

buildings and think it deserves to be used more in domestic spaces.

With more than a nod to the water that divides us from America, I also created concrete stepping pads across the pond. As you step into the garden, the first slab of concrete that crosses over the water is deliberately placed – making you maybe just a little uncomfortable – just enough to make you take care as you cross.

Again, I wanted to create a moment where you have to pause and take stock, not just walk straight across. I wanted the owners of this garden to be able to put their hands or feet in the pond, which runs around the garden in an L-shape. I wanted then to touch the water and be part of it.

At the very back of the garden, a monumental slab of concrete stands upright, forming the backdrop for a huge wall of water that falls into a calm, pebble-lined

Light and reflection really brought another dimension to the garden

*Shadows play upon the
polished concrete, adding to
the coolness of the space*

pool. After all, this garden had to have falling water!

As with Realistic Retreat and A Welcome Sight, I wanted the sound of water to be a key element to this garden because the sound was intrinsic to the atmosphere of Fallingwater – where it pervades the entire house. Wright is said to have told Edgar Kaufmann, the owner of Fallingwater "I want you to be of the water, live with the waterfall, not just to look at it."

There is nothing purer than the combination of woodland and water and here I recreated the cool green atmosphere of woodland that surrounds Fallingwater, using *Zelcova serrata* for the trees and Carpinus hedging to give a green backdrop to the garden. Most of all, this garden is about combining the built environment and nature. It's hardly possible to get a more man-made material than concrete and yet the polished slabs work beautifully with the planting.

Concrete is something that, in my opinion, we still don't use well in this country. It doesn't have to be sad slabs of grey. There are many ways of treating it, or moulding it, so that it looks natural, yet retains its essential essence of being man-made. It can have a stone-like quality – but without the joins!

The overall effect is complemented by a restrained palette of plants that play with shapes, textures and soft colour to create a haven of calm and seclusion. The Carpinus and Zelkova create height and structure,

*The concrete water wall sits between the tightly
clipped hornbeam hedge, whilst the stepping stone
over the water gives the impression of floating*

*Soft, lush planting contrasts
with the architectural
concrete pads*

balanced by the softness of the herbaceous planting underneath. The delicate leaves of the Zelkova give lovely, ever-changing light and shade displays on the concrete.

The hedging is made up of thin panels – only about 150mm deep – and because they were shallow we didn't lose much space – so precious in a small garden. Clipped Buxus tables added green structures to the garden.

The hand-crafted seats, inspired by some of Frank Lloyd Wright's furniture, were built by my craftsman friend David Rawlings. They sit in front of the hornbeam hedge and are a series of triangles made from oak, with soft grey cushioned tops – echoing the colour of the concrete. They come apart and can be mixed and matched, either assembled to make a long, angled bench or used separately throughout the garden. They bring an echo of Wright-inspired craft to the scene.

A feeling of coolness and calm is created throughout the garden by using a basic palette of green and white with accents of colour provided by the blue of the irises and geraniums and warm pink from the Astrantia and Digitalis. The white and cream theme is carried by the Luzula, Carex, Hostas and Aesculus.

This Chelsea garden was such a pleasure to design and I was delighted it won a gold medal. I felt it was a fitting tribute to the work of Frank Lloyd Wright – particularly as the people who came over from the Wright Foundation loved it too.

*The concrete slabs provide
a wonderful surface for the
sunlight to play on*

Frank Lloyd Wright and Fallingwater

Wright designed Fallingwater for the businessman and philanthropist, Edgar J Kauffmann, whose son, Edgar Kauffmann Jnr., was apprenticed to Wright at his offices in Taliesin, Iowa. Edgar Jnr convinced his father that he should get Wright to design the family's summer retreat at Bear Run in rural Pennsylvania. When asked by Wright where he liked to sit in amongst all those acres, Kaufmann senior said he had a special place where he went to think; on a rock ledge at a waterfall. Wright surveyed the site and then all went quiet. After nine months, Kauffmann called Wright as he was in the area and wanted to see the plans Wright had said he was working on. In truth, there was nothing on paper although Wright had been working on the design in his head for the nine months. Two hours after the phone call, when Kauffmann arrived, Wright had put the design down on paper! Building work began in 1936 and was completed a year later.

Above: The steps take you down to a platform that floats above the water
Right: Fallingwater feels like it belongs in the landscape – an organic design

"Wright understood that people were creatures of nature, hence an architecture which conformed to nature would conform to what was basic in people **"**

Edgar Kauffmann jr

Wright designed the house in 1935 for the Kaufmann family, who owned and used it until 1963, when it was entrusted by Edgar Kaufmann Jr, to the Western Pennsylvania Conservancy. Since it opened to the public in 1964, there have been 4.5 million visitors to Fallingwater

Luzula nivea

I have used this grass a lot over the years at Chelsea; a great working plant that really can hold a scheme together. An evergreen grass, it has dark green leaves with flower stems that carry small fluffy white flowers which are happy in sun or shade and will grow to 0.6m tall

Digitalis x mertonensis

This semi-evergreen foxglove has bell-shaped flowers, which are a wonderful crushed-strawberry colour in the summer. The plant needs moist conditions and can grow from 0.5m to 1m. Happy in sun and semi-shade

Aesculus parviflora

This large, deciduous shrub can grow between 2.5m-4m tall and 4m-8m wide. Happy in sun or shade. Can be pruned. A fantastic horse chestnut shrub; I love using it as a small multi-stem tree

Carex 'Variegata'

This semi-evergreen plant has broad, strip-like leaves that are striped with a creamy white and green. In spring, the plant grows dark-brown flowers. This tough hard-working plant is good in sun or semi-shade

KEY PLANTS
Zelkova serrata

One of my favourite trees, native to Japan and China and belonging to the elm family. It has lovely, smooth, grey bark and oblong-ovate leaves that turn orange in autumn

KEY PLANTS
Dryopteris filix-mas

This is a wonderfully robust fern that will tolerate strong sun if the soil is damp. Will grow to 1.5m in the right conditions

KEY PLANTS
Rodgersia aesculifolia

This large moisture-loving perennial has handsome chestnut-like leaves, which in summer carry small cream or pink star-shaped flowers. A robust plant that will grow up to 1.5m

KEY PLANTS
Hosta 'Francee'

This is a favourite of mine. It has green leaves with a good white edge and pale lavender flowers in summer. Happy in semi-shade or full shade in moist soil

Garden layout

Inspired by Frank Lloyd Wright and Fallingwater, the garden was about distilling his ideas. Water was a very important element in this garden, used as a space and also a reflective surface, as was the concrete.

As you enter the garden, you cross the water, with the water wall to your right which provides a fantastic sound. The design was really worked up from creating simple changes of levels across the space.

The steel trays were fitted with ground concrete to expose the aggregate, then polished to create a nice finish and surface that felt great under bare feet.

Crafted stools inspired by Wright's furniture could be used around the garden. The slabs looked as if they were floating on the water, creating a simple but cool space.

An L-shape pool wrapped the paving and reflected the trees above.

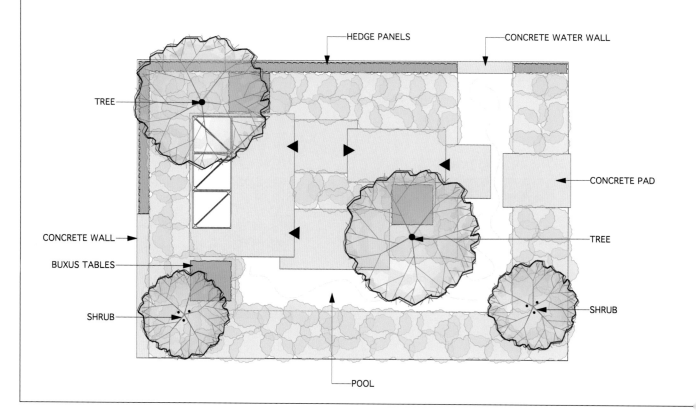

HEDGE PANELS

CONCRETE WATER WALL

TREE

CONCRETE PAD

CONCRETE WALL

TREE

BUXUS TABLES

SHRUB

SHRUB

POOL

Slabs and pool

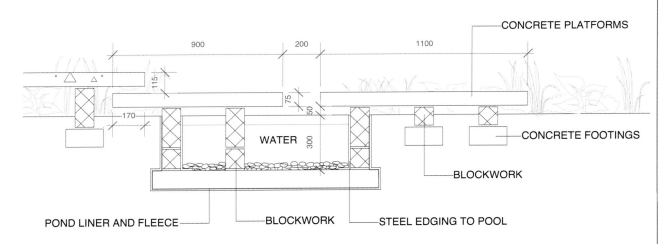

CONCRETE PLATFORMS

900　　　200　　　1100

115

75

50

170

WATER　300

CONCRETE FOOTINGS

BLOCKWORK

POND LINER AND FLEECE — BLOCKWORK — STEEL EDGING TO POOL

 SECTION VIEW

Water wall

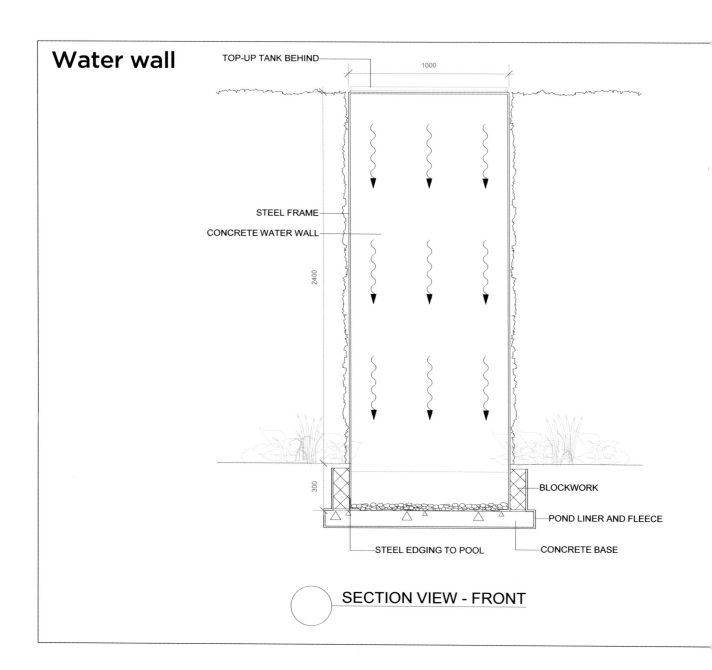

TOP-UP TANK BEHIND

1000

STEEL FRAME

CONCRETE WATER WALL

2400

300

BLOCKWORK

POND LINER AND FLEECE

STEEL EDGING TO POOL

CONCRETE BASE

SECTION VIEW - FRONT

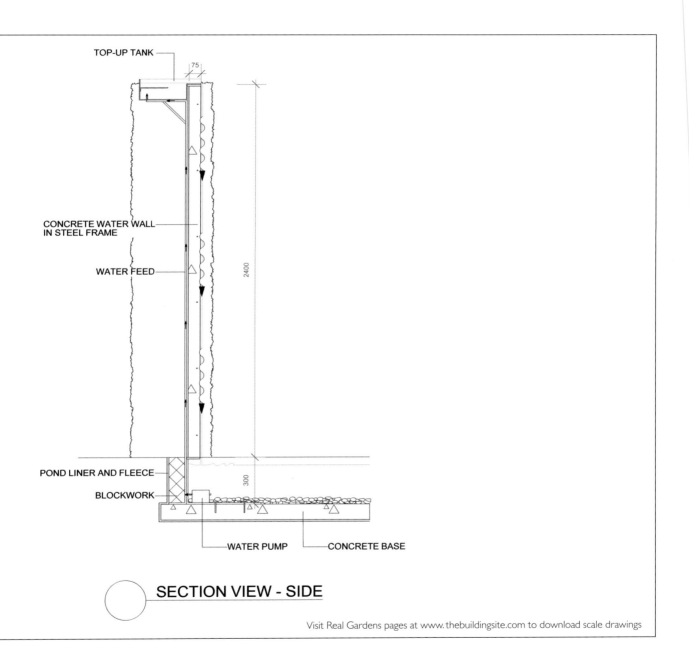

TOP-UP TANK

75

CONCRETE WATER WALL
IN STEEL FRAME

WATER FEED

2400

POND LINER AND FLEECE

BLOCKWORK

300

WATER PUMP   CONCRETE BASE

SECTION VIEW - SIDE

A Rural Muse

Category: Show garden
Award: Gold medal

This garden takes its title from a collection of poetry by the 'peasant poet' John Clare. I feel a very strong affinity with Clare; he was one of the earliest environmental campaigners and was local to me, living most of his life in the village of Helpston, just outside Stamford. Clare had a deep and abiding love of the English countryside. He was a direct contemporary of Keats and, in fact, his first book of poetry, *Poems Descriptive of Rural Life and Scenery*, outsold that of his rival.

Clare's story was one of poverty, illness and upheaval. He was of the generation that witnessed the effects of the industrial revolution, when the old, manual ways of farming and manufacturing were changed forever. Clare openly questioned the enclosure laws that saw common land taken into private ownership and also challenged methods of farming.

"Clare was always torn between the literary world, the countryside and the people he loved to write about "

Born in 1793, he was the son of humble and semi-literate parents and, although he did receive some formal schooling, his education was completed by the age of twelve. He worked as a labourer on local farms and even, for a brief spell, as a gardener on the Burghley estate near Stamford. The story goes that he slept in the summerhouse there but ran away because he didn't like the head gardener.

His early success gained him a firm circle of supporters in London. But he was always torn between the literary world, the countryside and the people he loved to write about. Above all it was his ability to share his thoughts and experiences in his poetry that have seen him rediscovered over the past 100 years after a period of publishing obscurity. He spent the last years of his life in and out of an asylum, although he continued to write magnificent poetry until he died aged seventy.

I see Clare as a lost soul, struggling to make a living and never fully at ease unless he was roaming the countryside and observing nature in the most minute

Stepping stones lead across the dyke and down into the arbour

"I wanted to replicate that special dark woodland feel under the canopy of the trees"

and forensic detail.

He became increasingly deluded about life as he grew older but maintained an astonishing clarity when writing about nature and wildlife. His drive to connect with the natural world around him – and to capture it in writing – was fuelled, not by learning, but by some instinctive ability.

The brief I gave myself for this garden was to create a space for someone who had been inspired by their local landscape. I took my inspiration from six well-known local Clare walks around Helpston. These walks literally start at Clare's cottage which sits in an incredibly diverse piece of countryside. If you take the route directly in front of the cottage, you enter a land of flat, stark fenland, with its vast open skies and long, straight dykes; out the back way, there are woodlands and hollows and gentle undulations with old limestone quarries and wild Lady Slipper orchids.

Turning right out of the cottage garden you enter bluebell woods, while turning left takes you to

Stepping stones take you across the dyke and channel through the natural planting, which is inspired by the look of a Dyke bank

Aruncus, luzula and geranium sit under salix stumps which all add to the natural feel of the garden

Limestone boulders create stepping stones across the water

Natural limestone boulders create a pathway through the planting

Stamford and to the entirely different habitat of the Hole In The Wall pub, where Clare used to drink. Whichever direction you take, you feel as though you are walking in Clare's footsteps.

The structure of Rural Muse is very simple. It consists of two parallel lines: one a rill representing the long fenland drains and the other the straight edge where farmers cultivate their fields right up to the woodland. This is represented by an avenue of hornbeam trees running the entire length of the garden. The trees create a canopy; I particularly wanted to replicate that special, dark woodland feel and to contrast it with the light of the open area in front. I was trying to imitate the change in light levels to which our eyes must adjust as we move from

John Clare:
Northamptonshire Peasant Poet

A personal appreciation by George Monbiot

The land around Helpston, just to the north of Peterborough in Northamptonshire, now ranks among the most dismal and regularised tracts of countryside in Europe. But when the poet John Clare was born in 1793, it swarmed with life. Clare describes species whose presence there is almost unimaginable today. Corncrakes hid among the crops, ravens nested in a giant oak, nightjars circled the heath, the meadows sparkled with glow worms. Wrynecks still bred in old woodpecker holes. In the woods and brakes the last wildcats clung on.

The land was densely peopled. While life was hard and spare, it was also, he records, joyful and thrilling. The meadows resounded with children pranking and frolicking and gathering cowslips for their May Day games; the woods were alive with catcalls and laughter; around the shepherds' fires, people sang ballads and told tales. We rightly remark on the poverty and injustice of rural labour at that time; we also forget its wealth of fellowship.

All this Clare notes in tremulous bewitching detail, in the dialect of his own people. His father was a casual farm labourer, his family never more than a few days' wages from the poorhouse. Clare himself, from early childhood, scraped a living in the fields. He was schooled capriciously, and only until the age of 12, but from his first bare contact fell wildly in love with the written word. His early poems are remarkable not only for the way in which everything he sees flares into life, but also for his ability to pour his mingled thoughts and observations on to the page as they occur, allowing you, as perhaps no other poet has done, to watch the world from inside his head. Read *The Nightingale's Nest*, one of the finest poems in the English language, and you will see what I mean.

And then he sees it fall apart. Between 1809 and 1820, acts of enclosure granted the local landowners permission to fence the fields, the heaths and woods,

John Clare (far left) lived through the first industrial revolution that saw lands enclosed and ordinary people dispossessed. The Rural Muse garden recreated the kind of biodiversity that was commonplace to Clare and is now rare in the countryside around his former home (left) near Stamford

excluding the people who had worked and played in them. Almost everything Clare loved was torn away. The ancient trees were felled, the scrub and furze were cleared, the rivers were canalised, the marshes drained, the natural curves of the land straightened and squared. Farming became more profitable, but many of the people of Helpston – especially those who depended on the commons for their survival – were deprived of their living. The places in which the people held their ceremonies and celebrated the passing of the seasons were fenced off. The community, like the land, was parcelled up, rationalised, atomised.

Clare documents both the destruction of place and people and the gradual collapse of his own state of mind. "Inclosure came and trampled on the grave / Of labour's rights and left the poor a slave … And birds and trees and flowers without a name / All sighed when lawless law's enclosure came."

As Jonathan Bate records in his magnificent biography, there were several possible causes of the "madness" that had Clare removed to an asylum in 1837: bipolar disorder, a blow to the head, malaria (then a common complaint on the edge of the fens). But it

seems to me that a contributing factor must have been the loss of almost all he knew and loved. His work is a remarkable document of life before and after social and environmental collapse, and the anomie that resulted.

What Clare suffered was the fate of indigenous peoples torn from their land and belonging everywhere. His identity crisis, descent into mental agony and alcohol abuse, are familiar blights in reservations and outback shanties the world over. His loss was surely enough to drive almost anyone mad; our loss surely enough to drive us all a little mad.

For while economic rationalisation and growth have helped to deliver us from a remarkable range of ills, they have also torn us from our moorings, atomised and alienated us, sent us out, each in his different way, to seek our own identities. We have gained unimagined freedoms, we have lost unimagined freedoms – a paradox Clare explores in his wonderful poem *The Fallen Elm*. Our environmental crisis could be said to have begun with the enclosures. The current era of greed, privatisation and the seizure of public assets was foreshadowed by them: they prepared the soil for these toxic crops.

SCULPTURE
The Doe

Designed and created by Laura Antebi, this life-size wire sculpture of a doe provides a wonderful focal point within the shady woodland. Inspired by a family day out in the countryside, the wire of the sculpture catches the morning sun and adds a lovely, natural surprise

" I was trying to imitate the change... to which our eyes must adjust as we move from woodland to meadow 🗝

woodland to meadow.

The garden was built using two levels, with the floor of the arbour being lower, which meant that as you sat in the arbour it provided different perspectives of the garden. When you stepped up out of the arbour you found planting inspired from hedgerow walks using geranium, aquilegia, luzula, carex and anthriscus. There is a firepit in the centre of an area surrounded by boulders. It was constructed from cropped limestone and capped off with sawn limestone. The boulders doubled up as seating and was somewhere to sit and enjoy the evening.

This clearing would be the place where you could imagine Clare's villagers coming together to talk, eat and entertain each other with recitations and music. There are also seats under the arbour itself. You could also sit on the smooth coping on the side of the dyke.

The dyke was constructed from carved stone capped with sawn limestone and, to break the smooth line, boulders – which double as stepping stones. The point at which the rough boulders and the smooth coping of

The firepit is reached by a narrow pathway through the planting from the arbour

the dyke meet references the points where the man-made meets the natural in our environment.

The arbour at the back of the garden is a shelter, surrounded and partly concealed by the woodland planting. There is a limestone wall at the back of the arbour where you can sit and enjoy the view and catch glimpses of the wildlife. Built into the arbour wall are small openings lined with oak boxes, inspired by the dovecote that sits next to Clare's house, that can be used by birds and animals... or to hold a bottle of wine. Clare enjoyed a drink and I like to imagine

The oak and stone arbour not only provides a great focal point but also a social space

An oak bench under the woodland canopy provides another place to enjoy views across the garden

that if he were around today he would stop and have a glass here before going on his way.

The green roof of the arbour is made entirely of clover – a reference to Clare's poem 'To A Red Clover Blossom' which begins, 'Sweet bottle shaped flower of lushy red/Born when the summer wakes her warmest breeze'. (I love the phrase 'lushy red'; it's a great example of how free and imaginative Clare was with language). Bees and other insects love the clover flowers and the plant is one of that select group that naturally adds nitrogen to the soil.

At the end of the avenue of trees which runs in parallel to the dyke, is a sculpture of a doe made of

wire. One day I was out with Sulina and the children on one of the six walks, and as we entered a beech wood carpeted with bluebells, we saw a doe. It was a really still day and the lime green of the new leaves on the trees looked fantastic with the carpet of flowering bluebells. The doe was in the distance and we all stopped. She cocked her head and froze for what seemed an age. We exchanged long looks with the her before she silently vanished into the wood. Eventually my youngest daughter whispered, 'Dad, that was beautiful.' It was a special moment that I wanted to recapture in the garden.

The idea of using the deer took some time to come to me. I'd been thinking about a focal point for Rural

Sawn stone cap to the firepit – which is surrounded by gravel. After the show the firepit went to John Clare's cottage

Muse, some statue or a piece of artwork. I couldn't think of anything that seemed quite right. You never quite know where ideas will come from. But I knew, as soon as the idea formed that the magical moment of the deer appearing provided the perfect answer. After a little searching we found artist Laura Antebi, who makes fantastic sculptures using wire. By coincidence she had recently made a doe that sounded perfect. When I saw it I knew it was spot on. It had the same alert stance of the doe we had seen in the wood.

In a great act of generosity, like so many that seem to thread through the making of all our Chelsea gardens,

Hedgerow planting of aruncus, anthriscus, geranium and luzula

Laura agreed that we could borrow the sculpture for the garden.

All the materials used in Rural Muse are very simple – no concrete in this garden. We selected Clipsham limestone, local to me and therefore to Clare, to reflect the garden's regional identity. We used it in different forms: sawn, cropped and as natural boulders. Even the off-cuts from the walls were used in the bottom of the dyke.

The arbour is made of the same stone, together with green English oak. Although oak is more expensive than softwood it has so many qualities that are

Timber-capped dry stone not only makes a great seat but also a home for wildlife

Old and young: meeting the older generation of Chelsea Pensioners is one of the privileges of having a garden at Chelsea. At the other end of the age range my daughter, Amber-Lily, loved handing out flyers!

superior: from durability to the way it ages – turning silver-grey and showing the texture of the grain. It also needs absolutely no maintainance!

The jurassic limestone is largely honey-coloured but also has patches of blue. It is a beautiful combination. The juxtaposition of the rough boulders with the smooth limestone copings (see opposite) made a pleasing contrast.

Poetry intrigues me. It is the linguistic and emotional distillation of an idea down to its very

essence. Like a single malt, it is a pared-down flavour of so many possibilities and ingredients. For me, Clare's poetry captures the essentials of love in all

Inspired by traditional dovecotes, the arbour limestone wall features openings lined with boxes, making the ideal wine rack

its forms. There is too much complexity and depth in some poetry, but his poems are very accessible.

I admire his poetry for that reason, but also because its primary subject is nature in its minutest detail. I am committed to supporting the John Clare Cottage Trust, which in 2005 bought the Helpston home where Clare

The sawn stone firepit is surrounded by limestone boulders and planting, which wraps the gravel clearing

Dyke side-inspired planting of iris, aquilegia and luzula

spent forty years of his life.

The cottage is full of artefacts and examples of his work, and the garden is planted as it would have been in Clare's lifetime. Some parts of Rural Muse, such as the arbour, firepit and boulders, were taken from Chelsea and used by the Clare Trust in their cottage garden.

Using English oak for the arbour gives a natural and traditional feel

It's lovely to think that the garden has an afterlife, just as it's reassuring to know that some things from this extraordinary man's life have been preserved in his cottage. I may not be able to write a poem in his honour, but I hope with this we did the gardening equivalent.

The green roof of the arbour, planted with red clover, helps it sit comfortably in the space

Anthriscus sylvestris

A widespread roadside plant; the whites of its flower look stunning in early summer. The white flower really catches the eye against the green foliage. The best conditions for the plant to grow in are well-drained soil and exposure to the sun. Grows to 1m-1.5m tall

Geranium sylvaticum 'Mayflower'

One of my favourite geraniums. Looks great in any setting and grows to 1m. It has a small, rounded, blue flower with a white centre in summer and spring. It grows in well-drained soils and is able to grow with little exposure to the sun

Dryopteris filix-mas

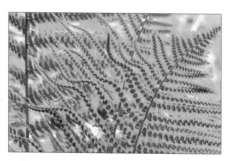

A fantastic hardworking fern ranging from 0.5m-1.5m in height and which doesn't flower. It's able to grow in most conditions, whether it's exposed to the sun or shaded and in a variety of different soils

Dryopteris dilatata

With slightly more fine-cut leaves than the filix-mas variety, I like planting them together. It grows up to 1.5m and favours sheltered conditions. The leaves on this perennial are dark green

KEY PLANTS
Corylus avellana

A tree or large shrub that I love growing as a multi-stem with broad, rounded leaves that turn yellow in autumn. In spring, this tree flowers with small yellow catkins, followed by a light brown, edible nut. Can grow up to 4m with partial exposure to the sun and well-drained soil

KEY PLANTS
Geranium phaeum 'Samobor'

This upright perennial grows up to 0.6m and has interesting leaves with dark maroon centres and rich purple flowers. The plant is able to grow in partial shade and moist but well-drained soil

KEY PLANTS
Briza Media

A delightful grass – its oat-like flowers look good in meadow-type planting. In summer it forms spikelets of flowers that hang from the green stems. It enjoys exposure to the sun and well-drained soil

KEY PLANTS
Trifolium pratense

This great little plant, commonly known as red clover, is widely used as a group. It has naturalised in many areas. This small, short-lived perennial produces a dark pink flower. widely used in folk medicine

Garden layout

Inspired by the typical fenland landscape of woodlands and dykes, the garden is very simple in layout. The boulders provide shape and movement throughout the space. The stone works well with the oak of the arbour.

The arbour provides a great focal point and sits you in with the planting. As you step down into it, the use of limestone in various states provides a sense of space, particularly when paired with the woodland-inspired planting.

The green roof, planted with clover, provides a haven for wildlife.

The detail in the garden really holds your attention. The firepit area created a different atmosphere from the rest of the garden.

As you move around the space, different views open up. Using local materials really brought a sense of location to the garden.

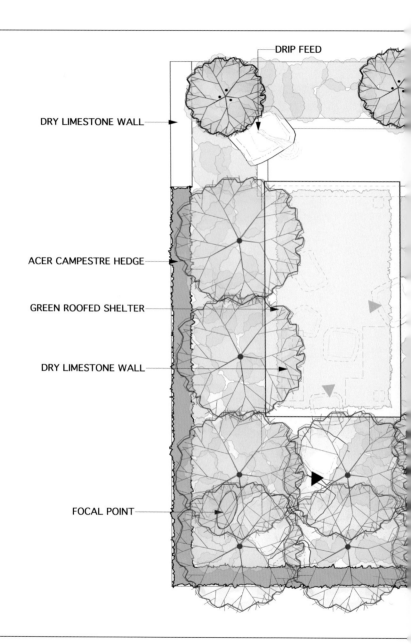

DRIP FEED

DRY LIMESTONE WALL

ACER CAMPESTRE HEDGE

GREEN ROOFED SHELTER

DRY LIMESTONE WALL

FOCAL POINT

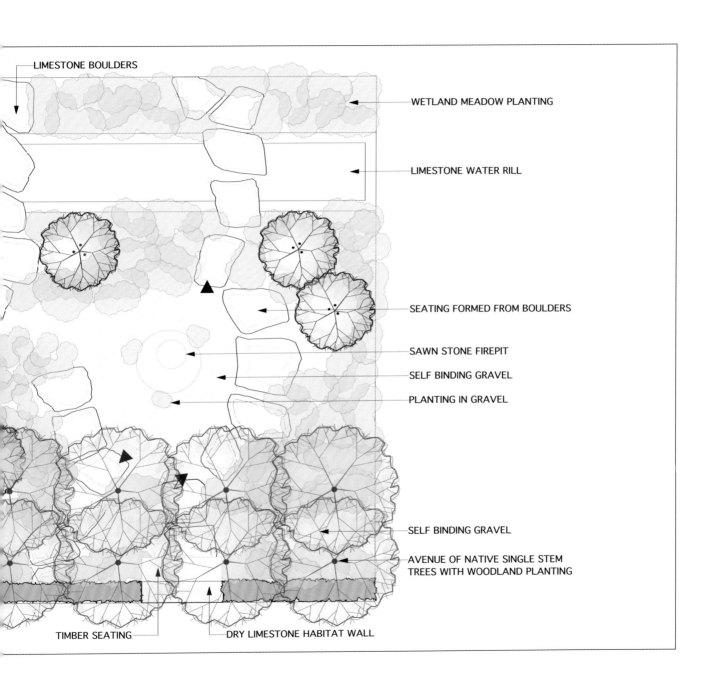

LIMESTONE BOULDERS

WETLAND MEADOW PLANTING

LIMESTONE WATER RILL

SEATING FORMED FROM BOULDERS

SAWN STONE FIREPIT

SELF BINDING GRAVEL

PLANTING IN GRAVEL

SELF BINDING GRAVEL

AVENUE OF NATIVE SINGLE STEM
TREES WITH WOODLAND PLANTING

TIMBER SEATING

DRY LIMESTONE HABITAT WALL

Arbour

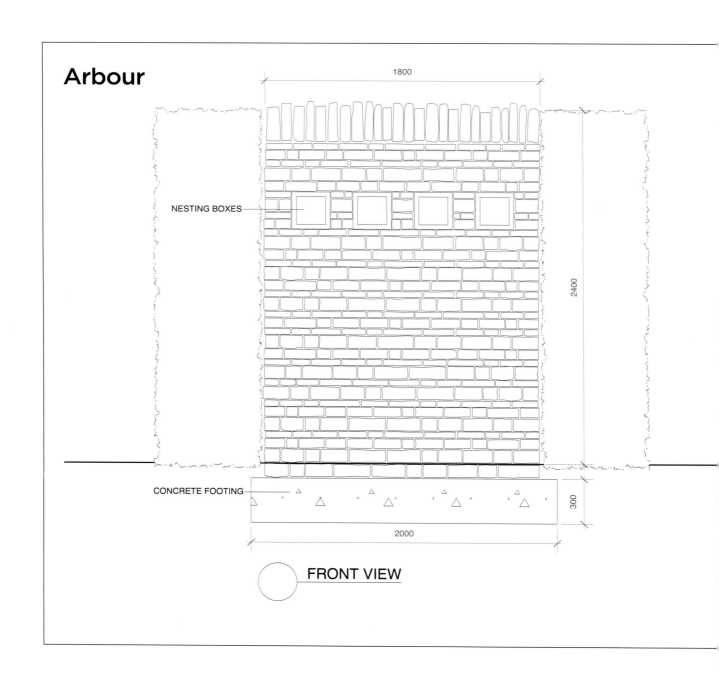

1800

NESTING BOXES

2400

CONCRETE FOOTING

300

2000

FRONT VIEW

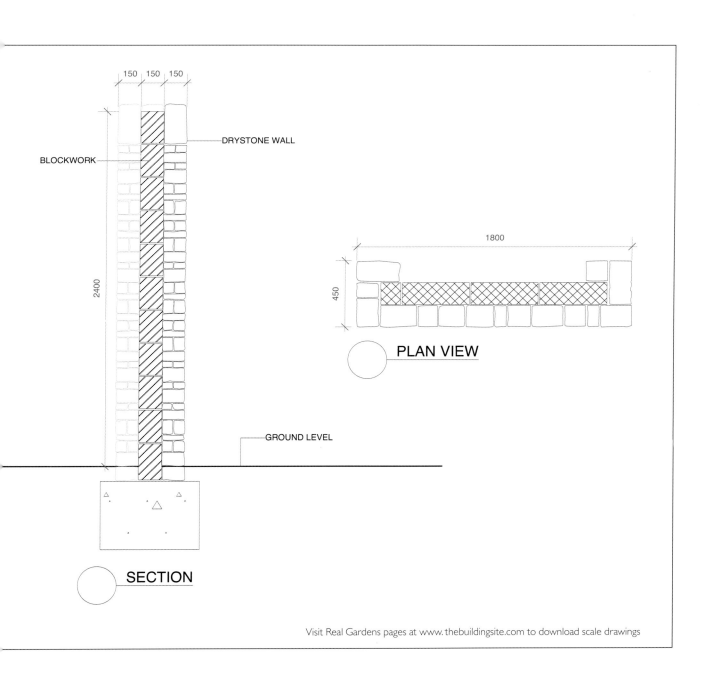

150 150 150

DRYSTONE WALL

BLOCKWORK

2400

GROUND LEVEL

SECTION

1800

450

PLAN VIEW

Firepit

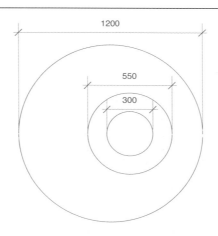

1200

550

300

○─── PLAN VIEW

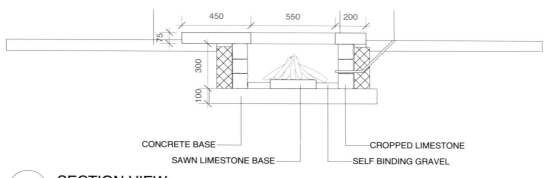

450   550   200

75

300

100

CONCRETE BASE

SAWN LIMESTONE BASE

CROPPED LIMESTONE

SELF BINDING GRAVEL

○─── SECTION VIEW

Water rill

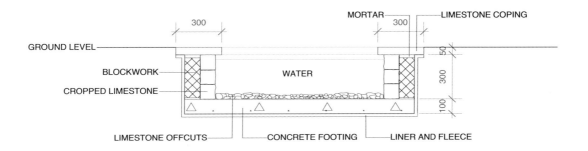

GROUND LEVEL

MORTAR — LIMESTONE COPING

300

300

BLOCKWORK

CROPPED LIMESTONE

WATER

50

300

100

LIMESTONE OFFCUTS — CONCRETE FOOTING — LINER AND FLEECE

SECTION VIEW

Gravel path

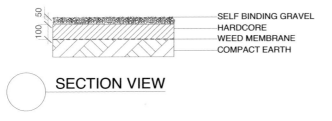

50

100

SELF BINDING GRAVEL
HARDCORE
WEED MEMBRANE
COMPACT EARTH

SECTION VIEW

Visit Real Gardens pages at www.thebuildingsite.com to download scale drawings

2013

SPONSOR: HOMEBASE

Sowing the Seeds of Change

Category: Show garden
Award: Gold medal

In 2013, I had a phone call from Homebase asking me to meet them for an informal chat about designing a garden for them, after my name had been put to them by my fellow garden designer, Joe Swift. In reality there was no informality about the chat that followed. Instead, I found myself face-to-face with a panel of suited people, all wearing the look that says, 'Go ahead. Impress me, and I'm not going to make it easy.' I was totally unprepared for any kind of formal presentation. I had worked up a few rough ideas on the basis that this year was the centenary of the Chelsea Flower Show. I started talking about the famous gardener, Russell Page, which, judging by their faces, was falling on deaf ears. After letting me waffle on for a while, one of the panel eventually suggested that

I design something around a 'grow-your-own' theme. I replied that I didn't feel it was quite right in the context of Chelsea, and it had been done before. Thinking I was digging myself into a hole I changed tack and talked about maybe updating the idea of an ornamental kitchen garden. Eventually, I headed home thinking that the whole interview had been a disaster.

To my surprise, Homebase called me the next morning and told me that I had been chosen to design their Chelsea garden. Apparently my idea of an ornamental kitchen garden, an idea born of desperation and developed spontaneously, had impressed. The idea must have been lurking somewhere in my subconscious just waiting for the moment to arrive.

I knew from the outset that I wanted to take a

The hops in the foreground, growing on one of three specially commissioned steel obelisks, are brilliantly structural

Marianne Majerus\MMGI

The shelf in the back wall of the
arbour is fitted with a rack so that
herbs can be hung out to dry

different way of gardening to Chelsea. I didn't want to build a classic potager, a traditional mixture of the edible and the decorative, which is usually in an area separate from the rest of the garden. I wanted to reinvent the medieval concept of growing edible and ornamental flowers together. You really don't need to segregate plants that are used in the kitchen. Geoff Hamilton had used this approach many years earlier when I worked with him at Barnsdale (that man was always ahead of his time) and I was going to build on this. My aim was to create a space which worked for humans and supported wildlife; a place where we could all feed ourselves and where we could teach our children how things grow. I also wanted to add a nod to foraging, so some of the edible plants were unusual and some were those commonly found in hedgerows. I replaced ornamental rhubarb with edible rhubarb, and ornamental currants with edible currants.

Although, at first glance, Sowing The Seeds looks like an ornamental garden, my intention was that every shrub should be edible. For instance, the hawthorn hedge that wraps around the garden has lovely white

Narrow picking paths allow the
garden to be tended. The paths are
made with Bredon self-binding
gravel between steel edging

Water trickles over the edge of the bowl and drips into the one below, and then eventually enters the rill

flowers in spring nicknamed 'bread and cheese' – because you can put the bud on the leaf and eat it! The matteuccia ferns scattered under the trees are edible, and the Chinese regard the hostas we planted in the garden's shady spots as a delicacy. In fact, I spent the whole week at Chelsea encouraging people to eat the fern fronds and picking flowers and leaves off the hedges for people to try.

My ambition was to create a garden space where a family could relax and reconnect with each other– putting their mobiles and gadgets to one side – but

also a space that was simple in shape and structure. Essentially, there are three unique but complementary areas giving a family a garden to suit their lifestyle. We placed the kitchen table into the arbour area which has a drystone wall as the back drop. The built-in-seating, oak table and bench provide ample space for a family. In the central space there is a metal cooking box where, after cooking the vegetables they have harvested from the garden, the family can relax and talk. Finally, at the front of the garden, there is an area of grass. I think we

The long gravel path provides a great focal point for visitors. Irises, geums and salvias are inter-planted with herbs and vegetables

The scent of the drying herbs adds to the pleasure of sitting in the arbour

love to see a lawn – I think there's something deep in our psyche that connects us with the most successful plant on the planet! However, this lawn is not for kicking a football about, since it's occupied by a large beehive. I wanted to show that there are more ways to entertain the children than just playing games; learning the names of plants, picking and cooking vegetables are great ways to engage them. The space is both functional and beautiful: a place to relax, to forage and to eat.

In layout, this garden is a series of rectangles linked together by paths that take you on a journey. The use of apple trees throughout the garden provides continuity and height, as well as providing the feel of being in an English orchard.

The simple rectangular shapes are linked together by three rills which double up as dipping pools. One tank was fed by the three small beehive-inspired steel bowls with the other two being fed by beautiful spouts from the end of stone seats. The three bowls are on the back wall of the arbour near the seating area. The steel cups sit in vertical formation and the water overflows from

The steelwork of the fire pit echoes the organic shape of the metalwork on the arbour. In the background the clay pots reflect the shape of the beehive

The steelwork on the front of the arbour is free-flowing and reminiscent of vine stems

one to the next. The dipping tanks were based on the memory of the old Belfast sinks which were a feature of my grandmother's garden, where as a kid I would spend hours fishing for newts, insect larvae and frog spawn. I had two nans: 'Tidy Nan', whose garden was a picture of orderliness and who even tied up her wild blackberries to the railings at the back of her house and 'Scruffy Nan' to whom the Belfast sinks belonged. Her garden was a wonderland of plants in no discernible order – not that either I or the local wildlife cared. Her husband, my grandfather, worked for Royal Enfield and Scruffy Nan worked in Whitehall. Although I didn't realise at the time, I suppose they were both quite Bohemian and artistic. She would give me lumps of clay to sculpt into figures and shapes and my grandfather would simply let me loose in his shed, where I would spend many contented hours just making things.

These memories are vitally important to me and to my sense of self, but it's only now that I realise these childhood experiences are the very foundation of the passions I have today. They formed the roots of my gardening career. Nowadays, I love to have my own

Artichoke plants provide strong architectural leaves and contrast with the iris, while the pear and quince add structure behind

UNIQUE ELEMENTS
Water spout and ceramic pots

The beautiful ribbed detail in the skep beehive was used throughout the garden – all adding to the sense of harmony. The ribbed detail appears around the water spout and again on the ribs of the clay pots. The bees moulded into the terracotta are a lovely feature, hopefully a reminder of how important bees are. The water under the spout is ideal for oxygen-loving plants such as watercress.

children with me in the garden. I never force them to join me, but they are always very welcome and I know that just by being at my side they are learning the names of plants, how and where they grow and the rudiments of design. I hope they will look back on these times and see the beginnings of their own interests and passions, whether they are garden-related or not.

All three areas of the garden are shaded by a canopy of apple trees. There are both main and subsidiary

(picking) pathways and both have steel edges to retain the beds. Dry stone walls with saw-chamfered tops double as seating in the cooking areas and near the water. The walls themselves are designed to be wildlife

The moving water from the spout in the end of the stone seat oxygenates the water in the pool below

The top of the wall was planted with the aromatic herb thyme – which can be used for cooking

havens and thyme is grown within the tops of the walls; a lovely aromatic herb which can be used for cooking or simply brushed to release their scent.

We used the same York stone throughout the garden, but in three different states: cropped York stone walls; sawn with chamfered tops; and shot-sawn York stone for the paving. Shot-sawn stone uses a course abrasive agent to produce a rough finish and is one of the oldest ways of cutting stone.

Breedon self-binding gravel is used for the paths. This is a mixture of soil and gravel dust. After it is laid, the dust particles settle between the gravel binding

it into a harder, firmer surface than clean gravel on its own. Using the same materials in different states gives a cohesive feel to the garden. It is a subtle kind of harmony that is sensed, but barely noticed consciously.

At the back of the garden, the arbour, table and benches were all designed to compliment each other. English oak is joined by a variety of custom ironwork. The table top and also the arbour rafters are supported by short steel rods that have been twisted into a spiral. Running between the oakwork of the arbour are curved

The arbour sits over the kitchen table - the borders were deep, but the smaller path (branching to the left) still gave good access

Plenty of room for all around the specially-designed table. Ideal when you have Mary Berry around for tea!

steel bars which have a vine-like feel. This vinery is echoed in the bracing that holds the bottom of the table legs in place.

All the timberwork in this garden was made by Dave the Boatmaker – as you may have worked out I love working with him. He is one of the most talented guys I've ever met. It's also fair to say that he's a little laid-back. Viscount Linley (who knows a thing or two about woodwork) approached him after seeing Dave's craftsmanship in one of my Chelsea gardens and asked for his portfolio. Dave is hugely gifted but modest, unassuming and unhurried; to this day I don't think

the Viscount got Dave's portfolio – he can drive you mad! But that's Dave.

The beehive on its York stone plinth on the front lawn is a visually striking feature. Most obviously, it is an essential habitat for bees, but it is also a source of food for humans. My design for the oak beehive was handmade by Dave, as were the bird feeders, bug house and toad den. The dipping pools are for dipping nets and for watching the wildlife.

The beehive really caught the eye of the public. As well as being a thing of beauty, having bees in a productive garden with fruit bushes and trees makes absolute sense

The lawn provides some breathing space amongst the densely planted beds and is the ideal location for the beautiful beehive

In the middle of the garden are three large pots, made by Jim and Adam Keeling of Whichford Pottery in Warwickshire, which echo the design of the beehive. Each of the three pots contain three ornamental bay trees, and are embossed with bees flying away to forage. There are also three metal obelisks planted with English hops.

The planting was probably the most complicated it had ever been at a Chelsea build-up. Show planting with edibles is hard work. Not only do you need three times the amount to use as it can go over so quickly,

but it introduces new textures and colours. I designed it to work from cool to hot, so started at the rear of the garden working with whites and blues. Then, working through the garden, introducing yellow and purple, and ending with hotter reds and oranges. All the time going along, working in veg and herbs so they sat comfortably. The repeated swathes of yellow euphorbia hold it all together and bring harmony. The rich colours of leaves, blossom and fruit also bring an extra dimension: the delicate pink of the quince, the shiny texture of the

The steel dipping tanks provide the perfect setting for aquatic plants and insects. The tanks are perfect for youngsters to pond-dip with nets

The steelwork in-between the oak rafters of the arbour has an organic feel – like the stems of a vine

currants and deep green-purple of the kale. This garden also benefits from the seasonality of the vegetables and fruit: rhubarb in spring, beans in summer and apples, pears, raspberries, medlars and quince in the autumn. Rosemary, thyme and bay provide year-round picking. I like to think that Geoff Hamilton would have been pleased with this mix of beauty and practicality. He would probably have said, 'That's not bad, boy'; high praise indeed from him. I know for sure that he would have approved of the hard work and effort that went into its creation. Without doubt, he would also have been as delighted as I was with the balance between

nature and wildlife and the culinary needs of a modern family. I think Sowing The Seeds Of Change proves that edibles can hold their own against the purely decorative. Hopefully, some of those who came and saw the garden will have gone home and looked at their own gardens in a different way.

In truth all I was really trying to do was take a way of gardening to Chelsea.

Peas climb traditional pea-sticks and the purple veins of the beetroot add low-level interest. Behind them, more traditional planting, such as roses, blends seamlessly

Angelica archangelica

A majestic herbaceous perennial plant that grows up to 2.5m high. In early summer it has light yellow flowers. It will seed about and makes a huge statement in any border or sits happily in woodland or wild planting

Matteuccia struthiopteris

This plant is best suited to grow when sheltered from the sun and in moist soil. It's able to grow to 1.5m in height. It has fine-cut bright green leaves that sprout from the sides of the brown stalk. A lovely fern which looks great as it comes to life in spring

Rosmarinus officinalis

This evergreen shrub is my most-used herb. I love the scent and taste. It can grow up to 1m. It also loves the sun and a well-drained soil. Makes a great low hedge.

Mespilus germanica

A spreading tree that grows between 4m and 8m tall and wide. It has white flowers in spring and yellow-brown fruit in autumn. It enjoys being exposed to the sun. We had one in our garden that I loved climbing as a kid.

Pyrus Communis Conference

My favourite pear; lovely juicy and sweet fruit in October with lovely white flowers. Tolerates most soil conditions. It grows up to 5m tall and enjoys a sheltered position

Hosta 'Royal Standard'

One of my preferred hostas, it has beautiful corrugated green leaves and carries a very fragrant white flower that appears in summer - not something you'd think would come with a hosta

Ribes rubrum

The currant grows to 1.2m. It flowers in April and May. The flowers are followed by lovely red currants that will ripen through July and August. Great for jam-making

Rheum rhabarbarum Victoria

Rhubarb grows up to 0.6m in height and 1.2 in width. It is happy in sun or part shade. Likes a rich, moist soil. Has wonderful red stems that are a sign of early summer. For me it is lovely cooked and served with ice cream, nothing better.

Garden layout

The design was really developed with three major spaces in mind: kitchen table; somewhere to sit and cook around a fire; and a lawn area with seating.

There was a narrative of water with long dipping tanks on opposite sides all the way down the garden.

The skep beehive detail was very important to the design, and inspired the spouts on the water feature and the shape of the pots. Steel edging is a detail that works well with the gravel paths.

Simple changes of levels are used around the space, with seating areas being raised.

Johnson York stone was used in three different states: cropped, sawn and shot-sawn – which provided interest and also continuity. The design was really created from linking rectangles.

Smaller picking paths divided the large rectangular beds, providing access to the planted areas.

The steel detail in the arbour was inspired by vines.

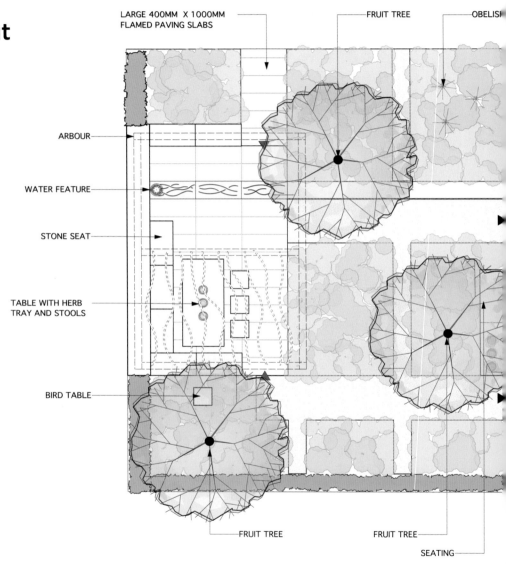

LARGE 400MM X 1000MM FLAMED PAVING SLABS

FRUIT TREE

OBELISK

ARBOUR

WATER FEATURE

STONE SEAT

TABLE WITH HERB TRAY AND STOOLS

BIRD TABLE

FRUIT TREE

FRUIT TREE

SEATING

DRY STONE WILDLIFE WALL

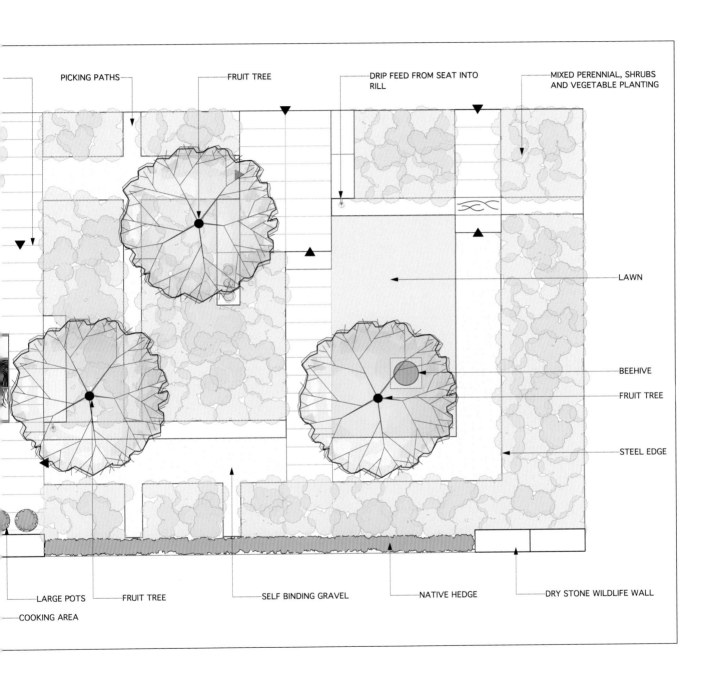

PICKING PATHS

FRUIT TREE

DRIP FEED FROM SEAT INTO
RILL

MIXED PERENNIAL, SHRUBS
AND VEGETABLE PLANTING

LAWN

BEEHIVE

FRUIT TREE

STEEL EDGE

LARGE POTS

FRUIT TREE

SELF BINDING GRAVEL

NATIVE HEDGE

DRY STONE WILDLIFE WALL

COOKING AREA

Table and benches

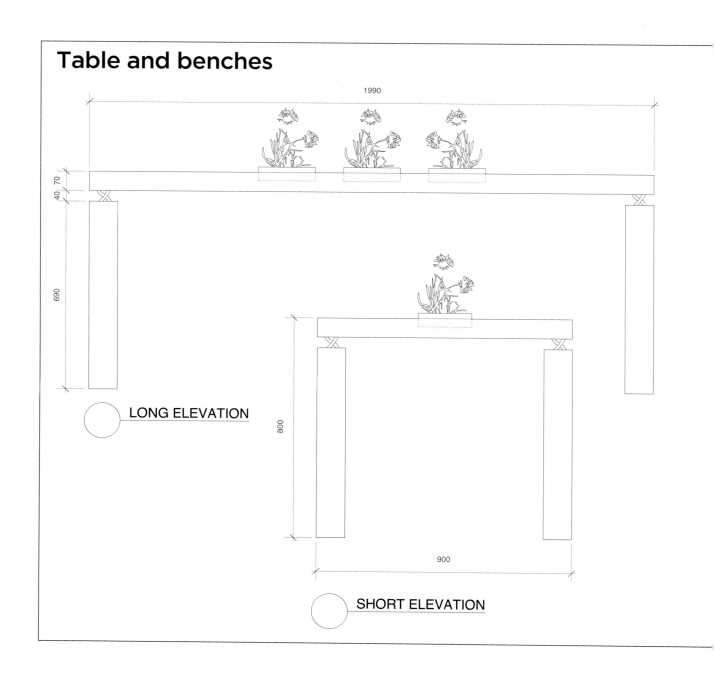

1990

40 70

690

LONG ELEVATION

800

900

SHORT ELEVATION

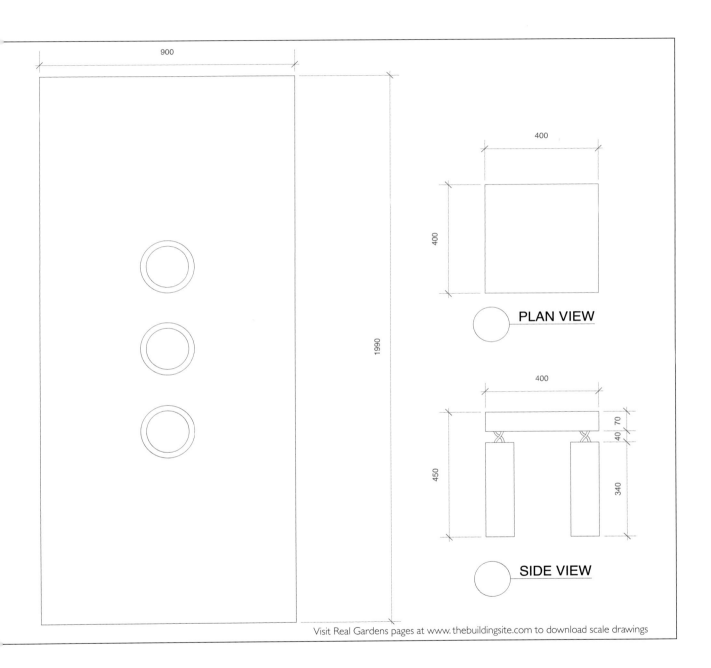

900

1990

400

400

PLAN VIEW

400

70

40

450

340

SIDE VIEW

REAL 155 GARDENS

Water feature

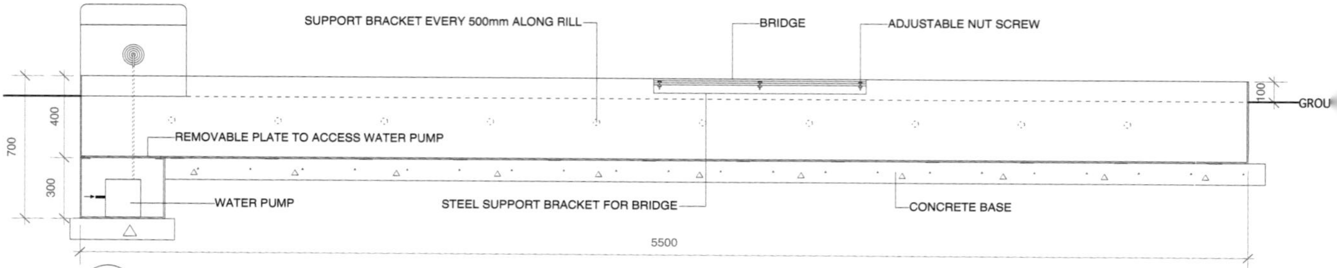

SUPPORT BRACKET EVERY 500mm ALONG RILL
BRIDGE
ADJUSTABLE NUT SCREW

REMOVABLE PLATE TO ACCESS WATER PUMP

WATER PUMP
STEEL SUPPORT BRACKET FOR BRIDGE
CONCRETE BASE

GROU

400
700
300
100
5500

LONG SECTION

ADJUSTABLE NUT SCREW
SUPPORT BRACKET FOR BRIDGE TO BE 10mm PLATE STEEL

REMOVABLE PLATE

400
2700
1000
1800
5500

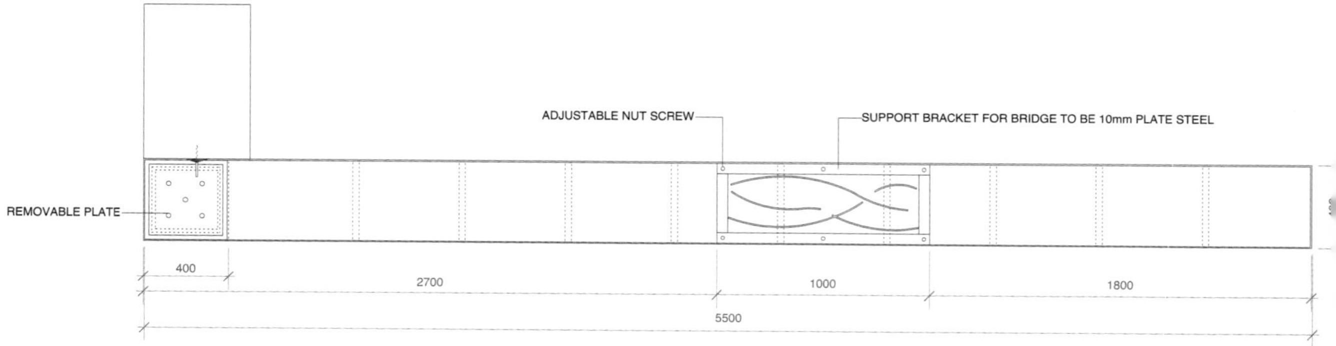

PLAN VIEW

Obelisk details

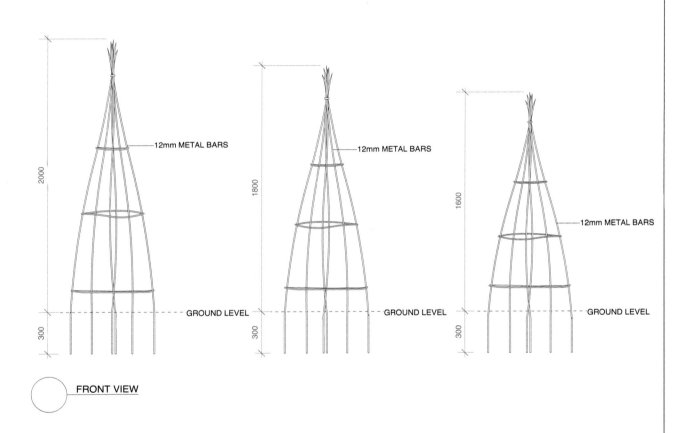

2000

12mm METAL BARS

300

GROUND LEVEL

FRONT VIEW

1800

12mm METAL BARS

300

GROUND LEVEL

1600

12mm METAL BARS

300

GROUND LEVEL

Visit Real Gardens pages at www.thebuildingsite.com to download scale drawings

Arbour details

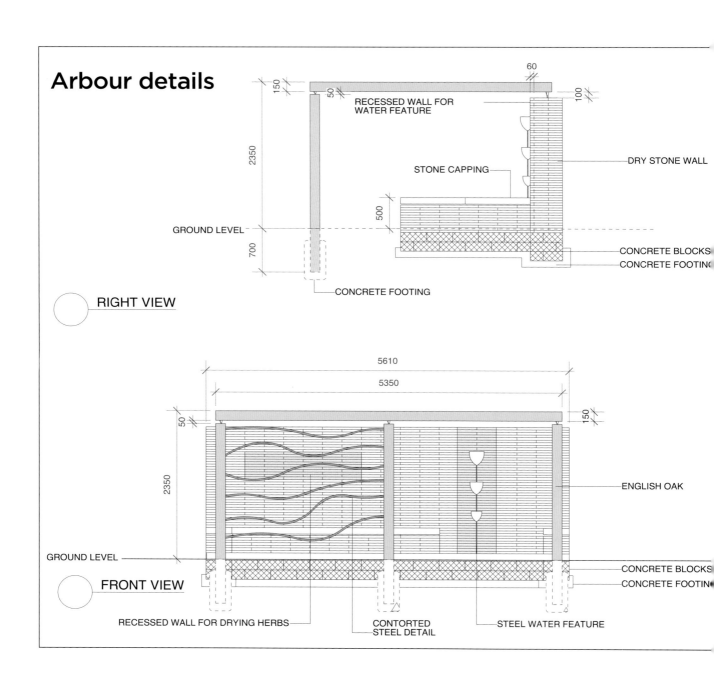

RECESSED WALL FOR
WATER FEATURE

60

150

50

100

2350

STONE CAPPING

DRY STONE WALL

500

GROUND LEVEL

700

CONCRETE FOOTING

CONCRETE BLOCKS
CONCRETE FOOTING

RIGHT VIEW

5610

5350

50

150

2350

ENGLISH OAK

GROUND LEVEL

FRONT VIEW

CONCRETE BLOCKS
CONCRETE FOOTING

RECESSED WALL FOR DRYING HERBS

CONTORTED
STEEL DETAIL

STEEL WATER FEATURE

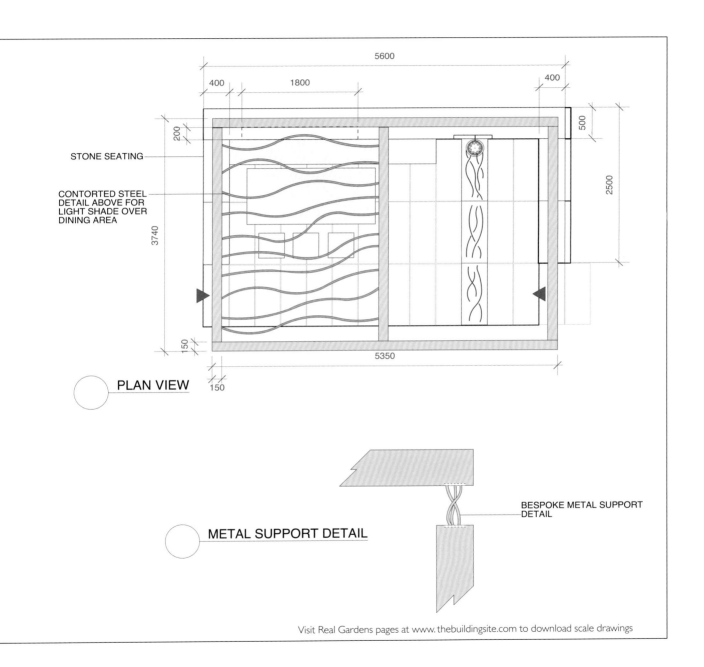

5600

400

1800

400

500

200

STONE SEATING

CONTORTED STEEL
DETAIL ABOVE FOR
LIGHT SHADE OVER
DINING AREA

2500

3740

150

5350

PLAN VIEW

150

BESPOKE METAL SUPPORT
DETAIL

METAL SUPPORT DETAIL

Visit Real Gardens pages at www.thebuildingsite.com to download scale drawings

Steel edge and nozzle

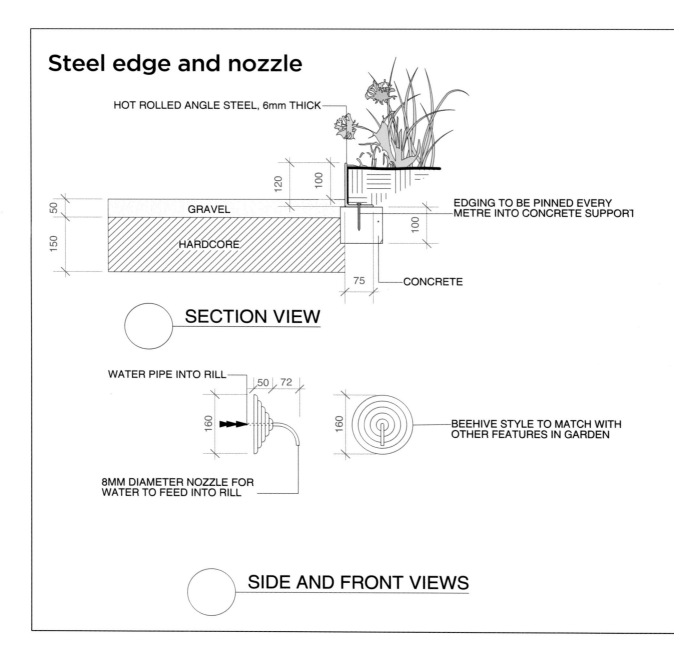

HOT ROLLED ANGLE STEEL, 6mm THICK

120

100

50

GRAVEL

150

HARDCORE

EDGING TO BE PINNED EVERY METRE INTO CONCRETE SUPPORT

100

75

CONCRETE

SECTION VIEW

WATER PIPE INTO RILL

50 72

160

160

BEEHIVE STYLE TO MATCH WITH OTHER FEATURES IN GARDEN

8MM DIAMETER NOZZLE FOR WATER TO FEED INTO RILL

SIDE AND FRONT VIEWS

Metal supports (table and arbour)

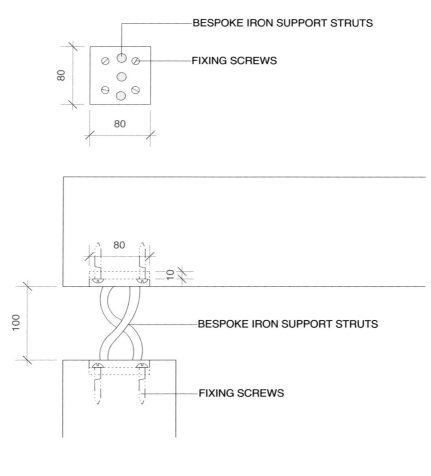

BESPOKE IRON SUPPORT STRUTS

FIXING SCREWS

80

80

80

10

100

BESPOKE IRON SUPPORT STRUTS

FIXING SCREWS

METAL SUPPORT DETAIL

Visit Real Gardens pages at www.thebuildingsite.com to download scale drawings

2014

SPONSOR: HOMEBASE

Time to reflect

Category: Show garden
Award: Gold medal

Inspired by memories, the garden is a calm and tranquil space to spend time with family and friends. An arbour provides shelter with a fireplace to keep warm in the evenings

This garden is probably the most personal of all the gardens I've created for Chelsea. Simply put, this is a family garden inspired by memories, providing a gentle space to connect with nature; somewhere to spend time with family and friends. Although it is based on my own personal memories it is really a celebration of all memories – reminding us how important it is to stop and reflect, as well as making time to create new ones.

Once again, it was sponsored by Homebase. But this time it was built with the assistance of students from the first ever Homebase Garden Academy that was set up in September 2013.

The Academy is really important to me and it came into existence as the result of a conversation, in a garden shed. I was talking about the shortage of young people coming into horticulture one wet and windy afternoon at Chelsea 2013 with Matt Compton, one of Homebase's directors at the time.

The Academy's aim is to help young people get started in horticulture and it was a privilege to work with a group of them on this garden. I am incredibly proud of them and their efforts. Nothing is more satisfying then helping enthusiastic gardeners get their start in horticulture.

All the graduates from the first intake have gone on to horticultural careers, ranging from landscapers to designers and plantspeople. The Academy has gone from strength to strength and is now in its third year. It's great to see apprenticeship coming back and

Water runs through the garden by way of a copper rill, moving past the lower seating area. The pint glass on the seat was a nod to my old man!

*Hostas and ferns love the
shade created by the arbour*

horticulture on the national curriculum.

Homebase also had a partnership with the charity Alzheimer's Society and, in preparation for designing Time To Reflect, I did quite bit of research about Alzheimer's. The more I learned, the more I realised what a terrible disease it is. When you strip it all back, in reality all we have are our memories, which are

personal and precious. As I began to think about my own memories from childhood; moments and events that seemed so long ago came flooding back.

When I start designing, I spend a lot of time just thinking about shapes and ideas. Design is a practical and evolving process and you're aiming to solve problems in a beautiful way. And it's the problem solving that needs mental space. Some of my best ideas have come from when I have been cooking or walking the dog etc.

My preoccupation with the past, and the people who influenced my childhood and gave me my precious memories, was compounded in 2012 by the loss of both my father and my beloved 'Tidy Nan', my grandmother, Maud Edwards. She was a very important figure in my life and one of the people who introduced me to gardening. I used to help keep her garden in order when I was a boy. I built my first rockery in her garden and pushed my grandad's ancient lawn mower on their allotment. I was given my own area to use and marked it with my name painted on slate. As an adult, Tidy Nan was someone I'd call if I had a work-related issue.

*Limestone stepping stones
create an alternative
journey across the pool*

She couldn't necessarily solve the problem for me, but she would reassure me that I would find a way through. I suppose, looking back, she was giving me the support and confidence to resolve issues myself. She was a gem of a woman whom I miss very much and about whom my children talk a lot, with fond memories.

Thinking about memory and life and what's important led me to acknowledge that it's my family that motivates me to get out of bed every morning and do what I do. And family, from being a kid onwards, is what shapes us. Our childhood memories are probably the most defining.

My father wasn't the best dad in the world – far from it – but he was still massively influential in my life. He was a landscaper with a fascination for rock, stone and water and a deep love for the Devonshire landscape. Passions I recognise I share. In his later years our relationship developed – on a more equal footing. In Time To Reflect I was making a garden I think he would have liked and understood. Sadly, he never saw the garden, but I'm glad I made it.

Like a lot of my gardens, this one is rooted in my love of the English countryside. When I moved to Devon as a child we lived in a village overlooked by an old copper and silver mine. According to my father, the old mine shafts ran right under our garden and the thought of this thrilled me. Having said that, my dad was a teller of tall tales. Although I took the story of the mine to be true, looking back, it might have been another of his yarns. But it doesn't matter. What I am left with is a memory of that story and the influence it had upon my imagination. Using this memory as inspiration, copper is a theme running literally

The soft blue, yellow and white planting was inspired by wetland meadows

SCULPTURE
Oak ball

The ball sculptures were inspired by the shapes of seeds and were carved from old oak by local boatmaker David Rawlings to my design. The tree rings show the age of the wood and represent lines of memories. The smaller piece is looking up to the larger, like a child looking up to a father figure – young to old

"**The structure of the garden is based around three different landscapes: woodland, meadow and scree** 𝅘"

through the garden; through the rills to the copper fireplace.

The structure of the garden is based around three different landscapes, taking you from the top of the garden down though levels. The arbour at the back of the garden sits in a woodland setting, with a green roof of herbs and mixed wildflowers inspired by the Devon moors. In the centre is a buttercup meadow with water running through it and at the front an area of scree. Each area is on a different level, creating a sense of movement, and they are linked together by natural limestone boulders.

You can plot a journey through the garden by jumping along the boulders that sit both alongside and inside the pool. These begin under the arbour and move down through the garden to create stepping stones that take you over and through the rock pools. There is even one stone that I deliberately made to

These two ducks put a smile on a lot of faces when they arrived during the show. The 'arrow slit' in the arbour provides a glimpse of the garden beyond, like a shard of memory. The peaceful shade planting behind the arbour

"The rock pool was inspired by my memories of clambering over them on the beach as a child "

stand just proud of the water, like the one stone that always looks dodgy and that you mistrust to take your weight as you step across a rocky pool.

You can take an alternative route by following the limestone pathway which takes you from the arbour to the scree at the front. This path meanders revealing a sequence of views.

These different routes mirror the choice of paths we take through life – some straightforward and some not! As you journey down through the levels there is a view of the pool, or a view back across to the arbour. Hand-carved oak seats are carefully placed for people to enjoy fresh views across the garden and create an impression of being in the countryside.

The rock pool towards the front of the garden is fed by the rills and was inspired by my memories of playing on the beach as a little boy – climbing through rock pools. My old man was a better dad when we were on holiday so those memories are particularly poignant.

The materials I've chosen are all very English. I've used limestone in all its various states, from boulders

The sculpted copper hood creates a focal point within the arbour. An outdoor fireplace lets you enjoy cooler evenings in the garden

" There is a balance between the hard landscaping of the paths and boulders, and the planting which is very natural 🔉

to scree, to create a very natural feel to the garden. Ironically, even though I am surrounded by limestone in Stamford, I could only find the exact colour of stone I was looking for at Chicksgrove Quarry in Dorset, which is owned by the wonderful people of Purbeck Stone. It is an old quarry that has been reopened. I also liked its association with Salisbury Cathedral which was constructed of stone from Chicksgrove.

The pathways are made from slabs of sawn limestone. The stones are laid in a pattern which runs at an angle of 30 degrees across the garden. Single steps, made from carved blocks of limestone, run at 90 degrees to the garden. Each space – the woodland, meadow and scree areas – has a slightly different atmosphere. I like to think of them as forming different layers of experience and memories.

The arbour acts as the garden's main focal point and is built from English oak and limestone. The green roof is supported by oak beams set within the stonework, which gives the impression of the roof floating. The beams are dressed with copper.

Natural drift planting creates movement through the garden. A carved bench and natural stone boulder provide informal seating

Three wider pillars feature long 'arrow' slits, which hint at the past and give brief glimpses of the garden outside – representing fleeting slivers of memory.

The design envisages that the owners will cook, eat and socialise in the arbour. On the long wall, over the fire basket is a beautiful copper hood. Inside the arbour the benches are made from the same stone with an oak cap. The boulders that encroach into the arbour can also be used as seating. The spaces under the benches can be used for storing logs – with the added benefit of providing a habitat for insects. Birds too are catered for with feeders placed around the garden. Bees and butterflies also have a haven – this time on the roof.

Sat on the wall at the back of the arbour is a carved oak sculpture in which you can see the rings in the wood as a way of demonstrating the passage of time.

There is a contrast between the hard landscaping of the paths and boulders and the natural planting which is deliberately minimal in palette. You could see this as a reminder that when you strip away the clutter of everyday life, when the trivia is removed, you are left with the important stuff.

I wanted the planting to have a fresh but simple feel; the feel of an English spring (with blues, whites and yellows). I have always loved buttercup meadows. They are beautiful places which bring back memories of placing a buttercup under my chin as a kid to see if I liked butter!

The garden is surrounded by a hedge of *Tilia europa*

The roof of the arbour appears to float above the stone walls – creating a surprising feeling of lightness

"Multi-stemmed hornbeam is used throughout the garden to provide structure and create a feeling of sanctuary 🙺

which is great for bees (and humans), as lime-based honey tastes great. At the back of the garden are a further three candelabra lime trees.

Multi-stemmed carpinus is used throughout the garden to provide structure and create a feeling of sanctuary. Inspiration for the planting came from walks in the countryside with Sulina and the kids. Seeing the freshness of an English springtime with blues, yellows and whites against a backdrop of lime greens always makes me smile.

During 2012 while I was thinking about the garden things at home were difficult. Sulina was very poorly and I did think at one point that I was losing her! I don't think we really realise what we have 'til we nearly lose it. Life just moves on and we can all take it for granted at times. This period stopped me in my tracks and made me realise what was important.

Within the cool shadow of the arbour are ferns and hostas with white foxgloves adding accents of light. As you move down the levels through the garden, the planting graduates from wetland through to

The planting evokes an English springtime with blue and white flowers against a fresh yellow and green background

buttercup meadow.

I wanted Time to Reflect to be both a place to stop and look back and also somewhere to be reinvigorated and inspired. That is exactly how it was used by many of the visitors to Chelsea. Some people were moved to tears by the memories of loved ones the garden evoked for them. It was quite astonishing to see the way they reacted.

One precious memory for me that year took place on Press Day. The final 48 hours prior to the show opening had been an absolute nightmare! I even had to get special permission to return in the morning to complete a border. Plants had been laid along the garden ready for use. When we got back to the flat, which must have been gone midnight, I had a bite to eat with the lads then went to bed for a few hours'

sleep. As I lay there I had this reoccurring thought that the ground staff who tidy up ahead of the opening would have removed them. By 3.30am I was back in the shower and at the garden by 5. Thankfully the plants were still there!

It was an even more testing time as I knew something the team didn't – I'd been told by the RHS that Her Majesty the Queen would be paying a visit so the last thing I wanted was for it not to be finished! Could you imagine, the Queen visiting your home for afternoon tea and it's a mess! When the Queen did arrive

The beautiful covered bench halfway down the garden not only created a great focal point but provided a place to pause

Light and shade is important in a garden and when I am designing I am always aware of the shapes and interest it will create, changing as it does during the day and across the seasons

Shadows played on the paving
creating a sense of theatre

she made me feel like the most important person on the planet. I wouldn't have described myself as the biggest fan of royalty but by the time she left I was hooked. During our conversation, I told her all about the history and inspiration for the garden. It seemed as if we were the only people in the showground. I felt so relaxed that apparently, as the Queen left the garden, I said 'ta-ta' – it felt as if I was saying bye to my nan, who would've loved telling her friends about me meeting Her Majesty. My old mate Jim Buttress, who helped me plant many of my gardens, had worked for the Queen in the past and he just shook his head and smiled as he was told the story.

It was a positive moment in what had been a draining (but ultimately uplifting) experience. Emotionally, it was one of the toughest gardens I created at Chelsea because the thought process took me back to a painful time in 2012: my Nan died in January; I nearly lost my wife, Sulina, in June; and my old man died in September. It was all still quite raw and as I'm someone that usually tries not to go back over the past, it was a difficult experience for me. Although it was painful at times, it was also cathartic, allowing me to both revisit my past and embrace the future.

Being in the garden led other people to reflect on their own experiences and that made it doubly special. That connection to the visitors is my overriding memory. Although Time to Reflect is very personal, like all my Chelsea gardens it was the result of a team effort and couldn't have been created without the hard work and support of the people around me.

*White **Digitalis** lifted the*
woodland planting, which thrived
in the shade of the tree canopy in
the area behind the arbour

Trollius cultorum 'Cheddar'

A great plant that looks good in natural planting. It favours partial shade and moist soil; its flowers bloom in late spring and early summer into a creamy yellow colour. The foliage is a deep green and it grows between 0.6m and 0.7m

Iris sibirica 'Flight of Butterflies'

This iris can grow in partial shade and moist soil. The foliage is a deep green colour and the flower blossoms into a blue and white flower in summer. It grows between 0.7-0.9m

Cornus mas

One of my favourite small trees, *Cornus mas* is a species from southern Europe. In summer and autumn the branches are full of scarlet-red cherries. During winter, the tree or shrub blossoms with bright yellow flowers. 2.5m-4m tall

Aruncus Horatio

A herbaceous perennial with fern-like leaves. These turn a cream colour in summer and light yellow in autumn. The flowers are small but come in large groups. The plant can grow to 0.5m high

Tilia x europea

This large tree is able to grow up to 30m tall and wider than 8m – though can be controlled. They have a slightly heart-shaped leaf and clusters of dark yellow flowers in summer. It likes to be sheltered from full sun

Astrantia major 'Star of Billion'

A wonderful clump-forming perennial with white, paper-like flowers which appear in May to June time. The plant grows up to 0.9m in moist soil and is happy in the sun or partial shade. It will carry on flowering through summer

Geranium pratense 'Alba'

This plant has relatively large white flowers, with rounded petals in summer and spring and usually all-green foliage. The best conditions for optimum growth, which is up to 1.5m, are partial shelter from the sun and well-drained, but not dry, soil

Carex Sylvatica

This lovely grass is found in woodlands across Europe, Growing to about 0.6m, the leaves are a medium green and in late spring small green to brown flowers dangle off the end of the spikes

Garden layout

The design was all about memory and life journeys. Therefore, I really wanted to create a space that had a series of layers, with water moving through the whole space.

Setting the building at an angle provided the opportunity to create a curved paved path across the space. The boulders provided a second route giving a choice of paths.

The levels offered a change in atmosphere from space to space giving the feeling of leaving a woodland and walking down through a meadow.

Using one material in different states provided that sense of place. As did the copper, which gave a focal interest in the building. Having water flowing through the garden helped create movement. The design offers different places to stop and enjoy different areas of the garden.

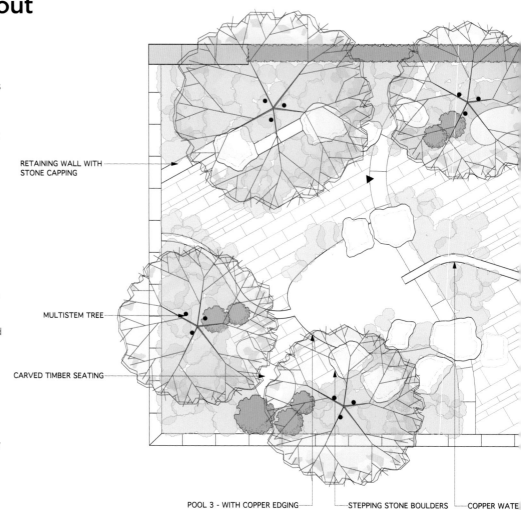

RETAINING WALL WITH STONE CAPPING

MULTISTEM TREE

CARVED TIMBER SEATING

POOL 3 - WITH COPPER EDGING   STEPPING STONE BOULDERS   COPPER WATE

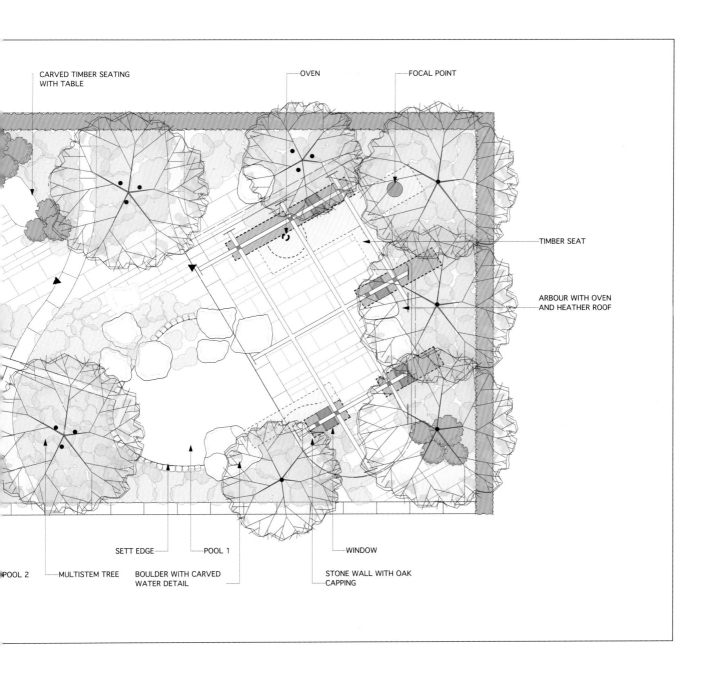

CARVED TIMBER SEATING
WITH TABLE

OVEN

FOCAL POINT

TIMBER SEAT

ARBOUR WITH OVEN
AND HEATHER ROOF

SETT EDGE

POOL 1

WINDOW

POOL 2

MULTISTEM TREE

BOULDER WITH CARVED
WATER DETAIL

STONE WALL WITH OAK
CAPPING

Tree and shrub plan

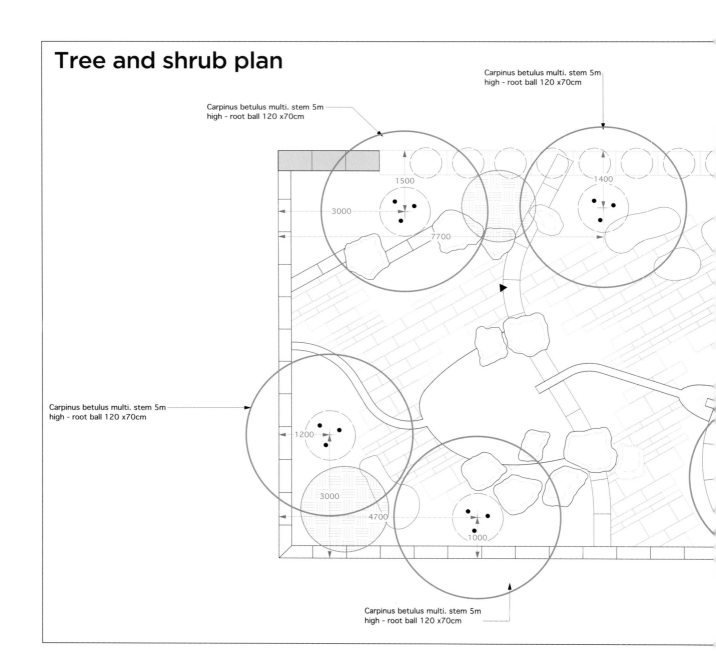

Carpinus betulus multi. stem 5m high - root ball 120 x70cm

Carpinus betulus multi. stem 5m high - root ball 120 x70cm

Carpinus betulus multi. stem 5m high - root ball 120 x70cm

Carpinus betulus multi. stem 5m high - root ball 120 x70cm

1500

3000

7700

1400

1200

3000

4700

1000

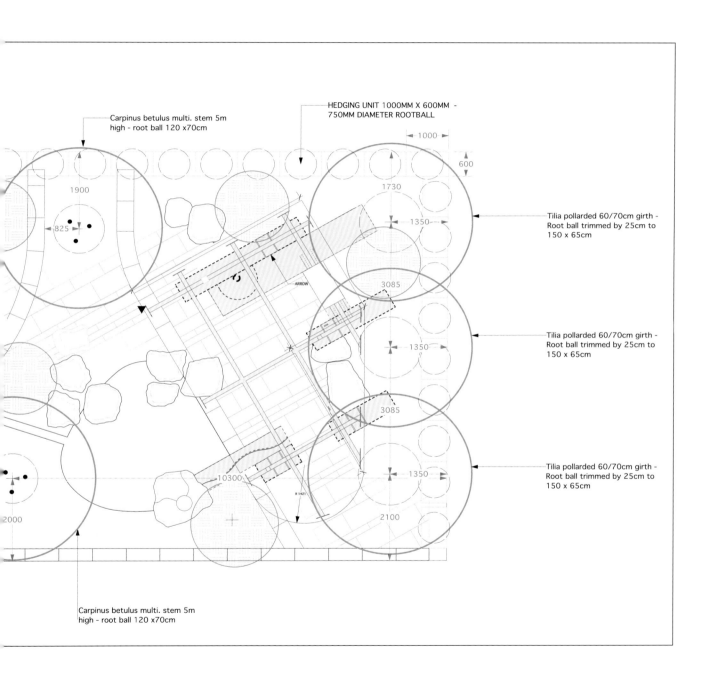

Carpinus betulus multi. stem 5m
high - root ball 120 x70cm

HEDGING UNIT 1000MM X 600MM -
750MM DIAMETER ROOTBALL

1000

600

1900

825

1730

1350

Tilia pollarded 60/70cm girth -
Root ball trimmed by 25cm to
150 x 65cm

ARROW

3085

1350

Tilia pollarded 60/70cm girth -
Root ball trimmed by 25cm to
150 x 65cm

3085

1350

Tilia pollarded 60/70cm girth -
Root ball trimmed by 25cm to
150 x 65cm

2000

10300

R 3421

2100

Carpinus betulus multi. stem 5m
high - root ball 120 x70cm

Stonework and arbour dimensions

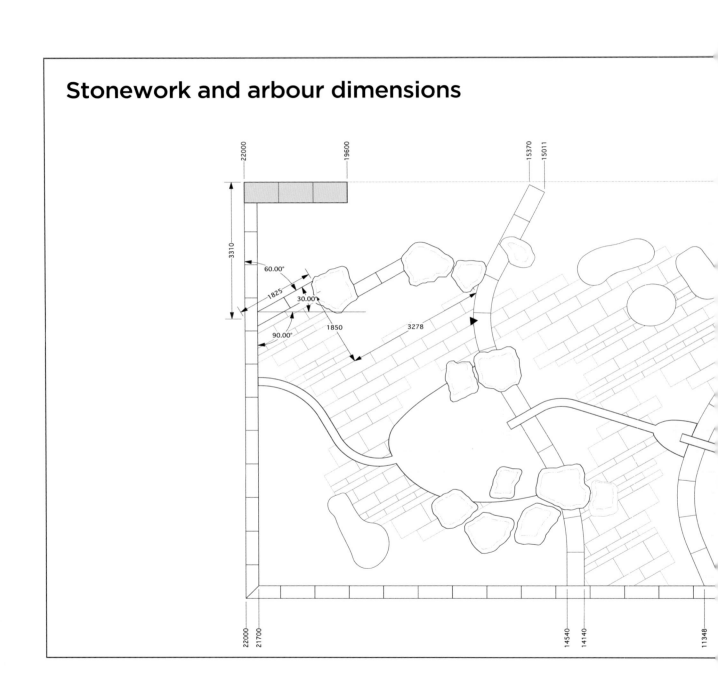

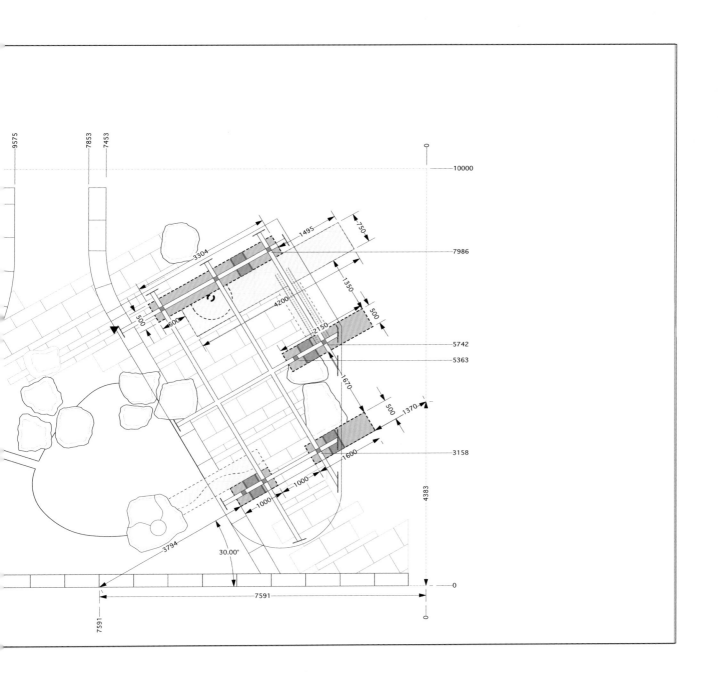

Step details 1

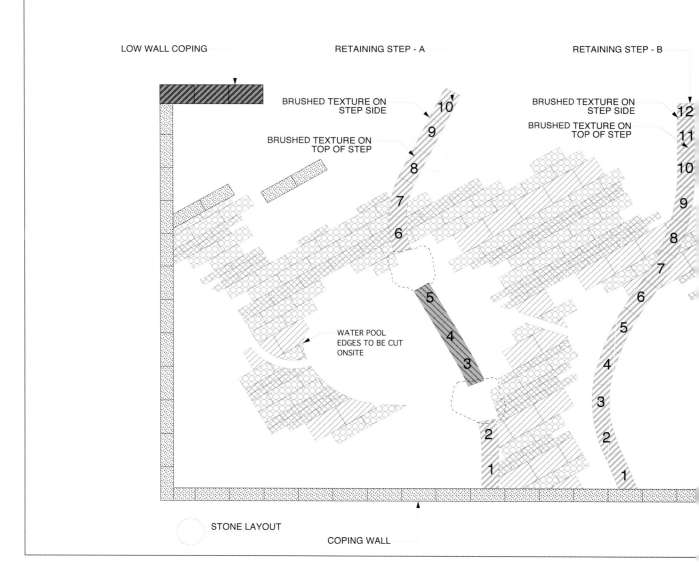

LOW WALL COPING

RETAINING STEP - A

RETAINING STEP - B

BRUSHED TEXTURE ON
STEP SIDE

BRUSHED TEXTURE ON
STEP SIDE

BRUSHED TEXTURE ON
TOP OF STEP

BRUSHED TEXTURE ON
TOP OF STEP

WATER POOL
EDGES TO BE CUT
ONSITE

STONE LAYOUT

COPING WALL

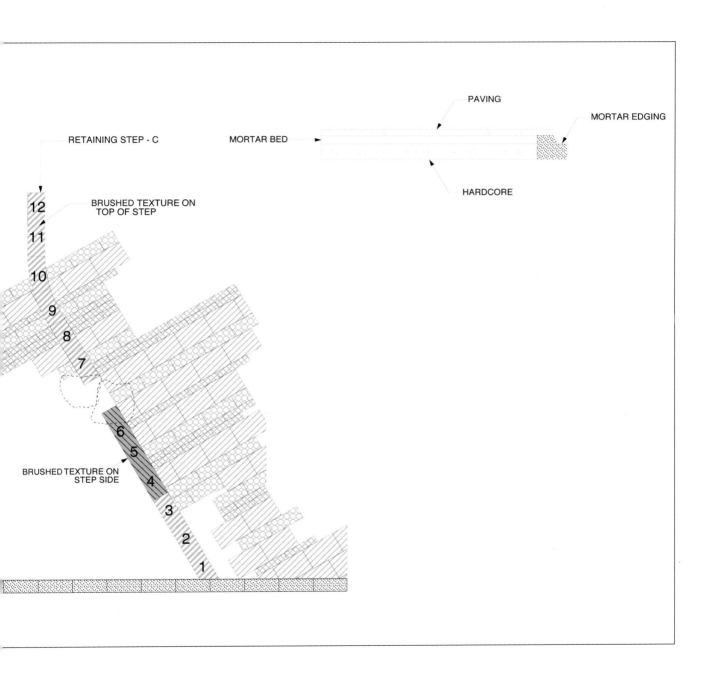

PAVING

MORTAR EDGING

RETAINING STEP - C

MORTAR BED

HARDCORE

12

11

BRUSHED TEXTURE ON
TOP OF STEP

10

9

8

7

6

5

BRUSHED TEXTURE ON
STEP SIDE

4

3

2

1

Step details II

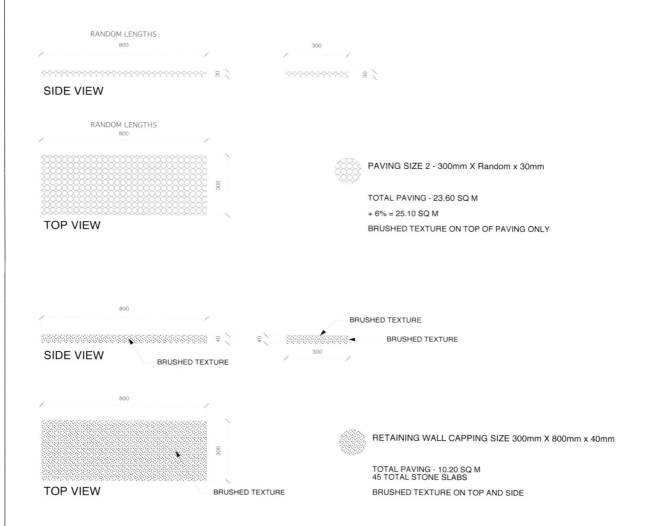

RANDOM LENGTHS

800

300

30

SIDE VIEW

30

RANDOM LENGTHS

800

300

TOP VIEW

PAVING SIZE 2 - 300mm X Random x 30mm

TOTAL PAVING - 23.60 SQ M

+ 6% = 25.10 SQ M

BRUSHED TEXTURE ON TOP OF PAVING ONLY

800

40

SIDE VIEW

BRUSHED TEXTURE

BRUSHED TEXTURE

40

BRUSHED TEXTURE

300

800

300

TOP VIEW

BRUSHED TEXTURE

RETAINING WALL CAPPING SIZE 300mm X 800mm x 40mm

TOTAL PAVING - 10.20 SQ M
45 TOTAL STONE SLABS

BRUSHED TEXTURE ON TOP AND SIDE

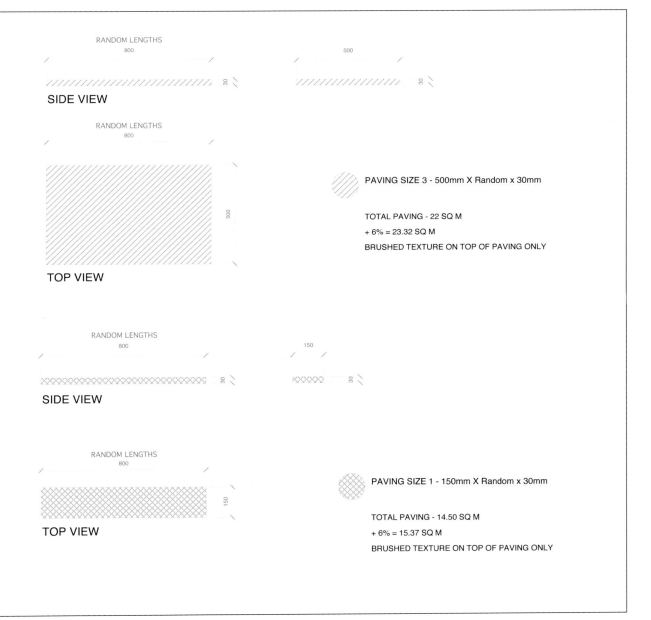

RANDOM LENGTHS
800

500

////////////////////////////// 30

/////////////////// 30

SIDE VIEW

RANDOM LENGTHS
800

500

TOP VIEW

PAVING SIZE 3 - 500mm X Random x 30mm

TOTAL PAVING - 22 SQ M
+ 6% = 23.32 SQ M
BRUSHED TEXTURE ON TOP OF PAVING ONLY

RANDOM LENGTHS
800

150

XXXXXXXXXXXXXXXXXXXXXXXX 30

XXXXX 30

SIDE VIEW

RANDOM LENGTHS
800

150

TOP VIEW

PAVING SIZE 1 - 150mm X Random x 30mm

TOTAL PAVING - 14.50 SQ M
+ 6% = 15.37 SQ M
BRUSHED TEXTURE ON TOP OF PAVING ONLY

2015

SPONSOR: HOMEBASE

Urban Retreat

Category: Show garden
Award: Gold medal

As I have said previously in this book, anything can inspire me to create a new garden: the glorious British countryside; modern design; a beautifully-crafted object; even a fruitful conversation or a great glass of wine! Inspiration is everywhere, and this garden was going to be inspired by architecture.

I love looking into history to inform the future. It's great to understand where we have been and why. When I started the design for 2015, I had been thinking a lot about loss of community and green space in our towns and cities, and how many grim, grey spaces there are in Britain. If I'm honest, it's a bit depressing, but to bring a neighbourhood together would be testament to the power of gardening.

I wanted to create somewhere to connect my community with wildlife and plants, something you may have worked out is a bit of a passion of mine. So, where was that inspiration going to come from? The answer was a movement and an individual that had long held my imagination – the design movement Bauhaus; and the designer Marcel Breuer. The two are fascinating and I can't help but get excited whenever I see an iconic Bauhaus building in all its concrete and steel glory, or feel the curves of Breuer's furniture designs.

"The whole ethos of Bauhaus was to create products that were simple in design and easy to replicate 🙶

As it happens, the buildings that characterise Bauhaus were often built around beautifully-landscaped community gardens – so it all fitted together nicely. Bauhaus promised a reunion of man with nature through community living.

The Bauhaus was a school of design set up by Walter Gropius in Weimar in 1919. The word Bauhaus literally means 'building house' in German. In a time of immense change and disillusionment, the school talked of embracing modern technologies in order to succeed in a modern environment. The whole ethos of the Bauhaus movement was to create modern products that were simple in design and could be easily replicated from the basic starting point of geometric shapes. The most basic tenet of the Bauhaus was: form follows function.

The Bauhaus Manifesto 1919 combined a variety of 'anti-academic' ideas, stating that mainstream arts, craft and design teaching were not preparing people for life's struggles (things that are still talked about today). Gropius called for collaboration between artists and craftsmen as essential and the focus was on the connection between theory and practice.

I would have loved to have been part of it! When you read the list of names that played a role in the not very big school,

The taxus domes follow the cedar path that winds through the garden, echoing the curves of the iconic Bauhaus-influenced building

Marianne Majerus MMGI

it is quite amazing. Its students and staff included Walter Gropius, Kandinsky, Klee, Feininger, Moholy-Nagy, Mies van der Rohe and of course, my favourite – Marcel Breuer.

Breuer was the Bauhaus designer who stood out for me. He designed the iconic Wassily Bauhaus chair at 23 years of age. It's said that the chair got its name as Wassily Kandinsky was the first one to see it and loved it. I also love that the chair was inspired from Breuer's bike handle bars (as I say, inspiration is all around you). It was near perfect, and the proof is it's still in production today.

He displayed amazing talent and, like Frank Lloyd Wright, was a master at producing great beauty from industrial materials. His architectural body of work astounds me, and not just the quality of it, but also the fact he had no formal training. There are a few pieces that really stand out for me, one being a house that he designed off Long Island, New York in 1969 (the year I was born) called Geller House II. It was a wonderful concrete building that had a beautiful curved outline of concrete that seemed to rise from the ground. I find the shape stunning and it played a large part in the design of my building for Urban Retreat. I loved designing the building; playing with a mix of concrete, corten steel and cedar was fascinating.

Another idea I loved results from when Breuer was asked to design a 'Garden City of the Future' to be shown at the 1936 Ideal Home Exhibition. It was commissioned by the Cement and Concrete Association. The scale model was made and, in the designers words: 'was to embody a visual presentation of an entirely new or ideal city'. He talked of the value of street life, the development of community and humanising the city, an idea that Breuer had been crystallising since 1923. It was a Utopian and schematic suggestion for the rebuilding of a city centre. I thought the

The garden's design is based upon a series of rectangles of varying widths, each one consisting of a single element, whether grass, water or planting

"The planting was designed with wildlife in mind, highlighting the importance of our green city spaces 🙶

essence of his thinking was quite beautiful!

So, with all that in mind, I set off to design an urban community garden that I hoped could be recreated in other locations. A garden that reacts to the urban environment and the buildings around it and rebuts the loss of green space.

The layout of the garden is inspired by Marcel Breuer's fascination with poured concrete, which helps give it a very modernist feel. Blended with that industrial, very urban environment is an idea that these spaces can also work as wildlife corridors. The garden was intended as a multi-generational space to be enjoyed by the whole community. The planting is designed with wildlife in mind, highlighting the importance of our green city spaces and demonstrating how man and nature can live together.

Drawing on the raw industrial materials favoured by Bauhaus architects, the garden featured poured concrete and steel. To that I added cedar, which bought a different, softer character to the garden; punctuating the boldness of the concrete and steel. Also, a long cedar-boarded path winding through the centre of the garden echoes the curves seen on some of the most iconic Bauhaus buildings. My design is based around a series of rectangles of varying widths; each consists of a single element: grass, water, planting – with one holding the arbour.

This building, towards the rear of the garden, not only provides focal interest, it provides shelter as well. The upper storey of the building gives a second perspective to the garden, looking down on the strong shapes and layout as well as giving views of the beautiful *Cercedphylum japonicum* trees. The roof holds corten steel containers, which are planted with wildflowers, providing a source of food for the resident bees in the hive which also sits on the roof.

The structure of the garden is provided by strong lines of

Corten steel structural panels on the arbour complement the red cedar used on the arbour flooring and cladding and contrast with the cast concrete

"The building was clad with red cedar which softened the structural concrete and corten steel **"**

concrete that break the space, creating the divisions; Taxus hedging compliments the architecture of the concrete whilst still providing good nesting space for wildlife.

Another favoured Bauhaus shape is represented by circular concrete pads that provide alternative routes across the water and stepping stones through to the shady area behind the arbour – where they are set at varying heights. Two corrugated corten steel water walls feed two long pools which can double as paddling pools.

The metalwork in the garden is made from corten steel – an alloy which has a rusty appearance but which needs no maintenance. I think its orangey colour gives it a beautiful, earthy richness which I reflected in the choice of plants. I must confess that, when the orange plants were delivered en masse, I thought for a moment 'what have I done?', but I believe they really did pull the garden together.

The building was clad with red cedar, which softened the concrete and steel. Inside the arbour, two Bauhaus chairs provided a comfortable perch, as did a seating-well with back cushions. The building was not only immensely solid, it was also very beautiful, with a cedar-clad ceiling.

Running down the full length of the garden, beside the

The planting was designed to complement the orange of the corten steel and cedar as well as the grey of the concrete

Inspirational Bauhaus

Marcel Breuer, one of the leaders of the Bauhaus movement and a hero of mine. His Geller House II (top right) influenced the shape of the building in this garden and I couldn't furnish it without using Breuer's iconic Wassily chair

hedge, was a concrete path at the end of which, just behind the arbour, was a corten bug hotel filled with organic material to provide a home for insect wildlife.

The planting in Urban Retreat reflects the colour palette of the man-made materials to bring harmony to the scheme. There are three *Cercidiphyllum japonicum* providing shade and a back drop to the rear of the garden. These trees have a browny-orange leaf and, after the first frosts of autumn, smell of burnt sugar or candyfloss. It's a wonderfully potent smell that lingers.

There are three more cercidiphyllum in the centre of the garden, providing a green canopy in spring and summer and a wonderful vibrant orange one in autumn. Taxus domes

The corrugated corten steel water wall adds colour and texture. The water trickling down feeds the pond which doubles as a paddling pool

"I wanted the area behind the arbour to be cool: somewhere to play with texture, light and form 🎵

bounce though the garden, creating great structure and movement. The circular cedar seating, inspired by Breuer's Isokon furniture, was created from layers of cedar, cold-moulded to form simple but beautiful seats, sat on slightly larger concrete pads.

The planting in the garden was chosen with wildlife in mind and my colour palette was bold and rich; through orange to crimson, highlighted with a splash of light blue. This not only referenced the concrete but also bought a harmony to the garden.

The irises, geraniums and digitalis sit alongside taxus domes which provide nesting space for insects and birds while the striking katsura trees (*Cercidiphyllum japonicum*) in the garden act as a source of food for the resident bees.

Behind the arbour is an area of deep shade planting as I needed this area of the garden to have a completely different atmosphere to the main space. I wanted it to be cool in feel – somewhere to play with texture, light and form.

I have tried very hard to keep all my gardens real. I wanted to move away from the catwalk gardens that have populated Chelsea over the years. This is perhaps the most real of all my garden designs and it is my dream that Urban Retreat will be used as a kind of template to bring beauty, wildlife and

Tree ferns, hosta, ferns and digitalis combine in a lush shaded area behind the arbour. The shade is provided by **Cercidiphyllum japonicum**

"It is my dream that this garden will be used as a template to bring beauty, wildlife and community spaces to our cities 🙾

Top left: The beehive on top of the arbour is flanked by corton steel containers full of meadow flowers. Above left: The cylindrical cedar seating was inspired by Bauhaus designer Marcel Breuer's Isokon furniture. Above: The cedar finish in the arbour provided warmth to the space

Structure to the planting was provided by euonymus and taxus; colour and texture was provided by hardy perennials

"It may seem hard to believe but the journey from design idea to finished garden takes around a year"

community spaces to our urban areas. With a bit of thought and imagination and perhaps the odd beehive, we can create shared practical places where people will love to spend time. As I said, I do like to dream!

Following this chapter is a photographic day-by-day record of creating the 2015 Garden at Chelsea that hopefully gives an idea of what goes into it. We live, breathe and sleep the garden for that month.

I have to go into schools and talk to young people about horticulture as, apparently, it's not cool. Some people believe there's no excitement in horticulture but, with a Chelsea garden, nothing could be further from the truth. It may seem hard to believe but the journey from design idea to finished garden takes me around a year. In fact, I start sketching ideas for the next garden before building is complete on the previous one.

The intensity of activity builds throughout the year. Both sides of Christmas, I was off visiting growers to check plants, hedging and trees. Those visits continued until literally days before we started constructing the garden.

Architectural in quality, the operation on the ground is like a military campaign. The planning has to be perfect or the garden just won't happen in the 19 days we have on the Chelsea Hospital site.

Standing on the roof of the arbour with the beehive and meadow grass provides a different perspective on the garden below

The Academy apprentices join in

The Homebase Garden Academy started from a conversation in a shed at Chelsea 2013 with a Homebase director of the time, Matt Compton. He wanted me to do another Chelsea and I said I wanted it to be part of a bigger story – whatever that meant!

Our industry had been moaning about the skills gap and where the next horticulturists were coming from. Matt and I chatted about this and a couple of hours later, the Homebase Garden Academy was born.

We wanted to bring young people into the industry and Homebase agreed to offer year-long training to apprentices. Four months after that chat in the shed we took on the first twelve students as a pilot intake. It was amazing. But then again, I knew it was going to work with the support of Matt and the team at Homebase – they were top-drawer.

The programme offers people aged 16 and above the chance to learn about garden planning and design, working with Homebase suppliers to gaining

knowledge across the board. As well as learning practical horticultural skills to earn a RHS Level 1 Award – and helping with a Chelsea Show Garden build.

After my own apprenticeship in Devon, I moved back to London to be a landscaper. I was then lucky enough to get a job with gardener Geoff Hamilton, and I worked with him for seven years. I loved what I did but Geoff took my interest to a whole other level. He was infectious – his passion for plants and getting people garden. He's left me with that passion and in a strange way it's transferred to the Academy.

It is a fantastic opportunity for people from different backgrounds and all ages to come together to share their passion for gardening and the outdoors and develop it into a great career. They go through

everything from learning how secateurs are made to spending time meeting with major growers whilst gaining retail experience along the way – you wouldn't get that in college during a twelve-month course.

The first year blew me away. So the next year we took on even more students. Twenty of them all came on the Chelsea journey again. I think it's fair to say they loved it. However, I did question my sanity at times: it's hard enough trying to create a show garden, let alone with twenty apprentices to organise!

This year we have taken on another 40 apprentices and are talking about probably recruiting more. There is plenty of demand out there for apprenticeships – receiving more than 1,500 applications this year alone!

Gymnocarpium dryopteris

I love this small oak fern, with its divided, almost triangular leaves. It grows up to approximately 0.3m tall with bright green leaves in all seasons. It grows best when sheltered from the sun and in moist soil

Digitalis 'Pam's Choice'

Strong spikes of creamy white flowers with a throat of the deepest velvet burgundy. This foxglove grows up to 1.5m tall, with the flowers appearing on sturdy stems throughout the summer. They work well in a mix of sun and shade and best in moist soil

Geum 'Marmalade'

A compact perennial with dark green foliage and burnt-orange flowers appearing in April and May. It can grow to 70cm and is an ideal choice for the front of the border. Prefers sun or partial shade and moist well-drained soil

Euphorbia palustris

A bushy perennial with bright green leaves, it produces small green flowers with a milky sap that turn yellow in spring. They grow well exposed to the sun in well-drained soils, up to a height of 0.9m tall

Cercidiphyllum japonicum

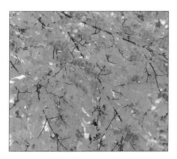

An Asian tree that can grow up to 12m tall.
It has heart-shaped leaves that turn yellow,
red and purple in the autumn. As the leaves
fall from the tree later in the year, they give
off an aroma like candy floss, Kids will love it!
I use this tree in most of my family gardens

Hosta 'Devon Green'

This hosta provides great foliage with its
glossy dark green, heart-shaped leaves.
Pale lilac flowers appear in the summer and
last several weeks. Growing up to 0.5.m tall,
it prefers partial to full shade with moist,
well-drained soil

Taxus baccata

Commonly known as English Yew, this is a
slow-growing evergreen which has clusters
of tiny dark green leaves, with yellow
flowers in spring. It grows well – up to 20m
tall – in any aspect, with well-drained soil

Iris sibirica 'Tamberg'

Flowering between late spring and early
summer, this iris has a stunning blue flower
that looks like dancing butterflies. Growing
up to a full height of 0.9m, it prefers moist
soil and full sun

Garden layout

Inspired by the Bauhaus movement, in particular designer Marcel Breuer, the garden really reflected the strong shapes in his work work. The space is a series of rectangles of lawn, water and planting. Spaces that can be enjoyed.

The choice of materials was very important to give a modern feel. We used corten steel and concrete with cedar to softness to palette. Outside the concrete had an acid-etched finish which made the surface really sparkle in the sunlight; whereas, inside the building we ground the surface of the concrete to expose the aggregates.

The corten steel really provides an earthy element to the garden and a great colour to develop planting; from the orange and crison, then blending in blues – which really brought the space alive.

The water walls deceived the eye as you only saw the water running down from certain viewpoints.

The area behind the arbour provided a completely different atmosphere. The stepping stones varied in height to make you more aware of your surroundings as you moved through.

GROUND LEVEL PLAN

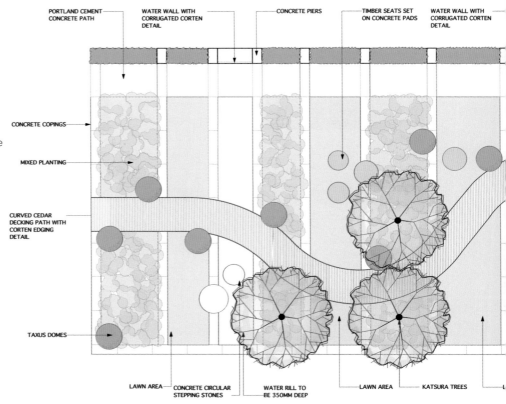

PORTLAND CEMENT CONCRETE PATH

WATER WALL WITH CORRUGATED CORTEN DETAIL

CONCRETE PIERS

TIMBER SEATS SET ON CONCRETE PADS

WATER WALL WITH CORRUGATED CORTEN DETAIL

CONCRETE COPINGS

MIXED PLANTING

CURVED CEDAR DECKING PATH WITH CORTEN EDGING DETAIL

TAXUS DOMES

LAWN AREA

CONCRETE CIRCULAR STEPPING STONES

WATER RILL TO BE 350MM DEEP

LAWN AREA

KATSURA TREES

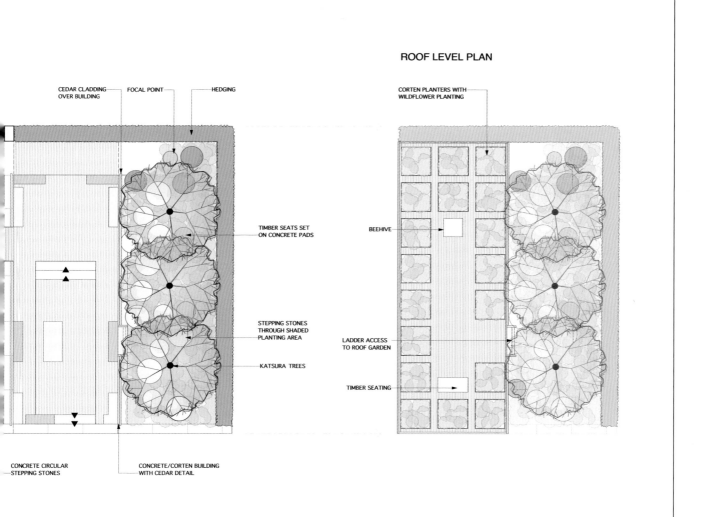

ROOF LEVEL PLAN

CEDAR CLADDING
OVER BUILDING

FOCAL POINT

HEDGING

CORTEN PLANTERS WITH
WILDFLOWER PLANTING

TIMBER SEATS SET
ON CONCRETE PADS

BEEHIVE

STEPPING STONES
THROUGH SHADED
PLANTING AREA

LADDER ACCESS
TO ROOF GARDEN

KATSURA TREES

TIMBER SEATING

CONCRETE CIRCULAR
STEPPING STONES

CONCRETE/CORTEN BUILDING
WITH CEDAR DETAIL

Beehive

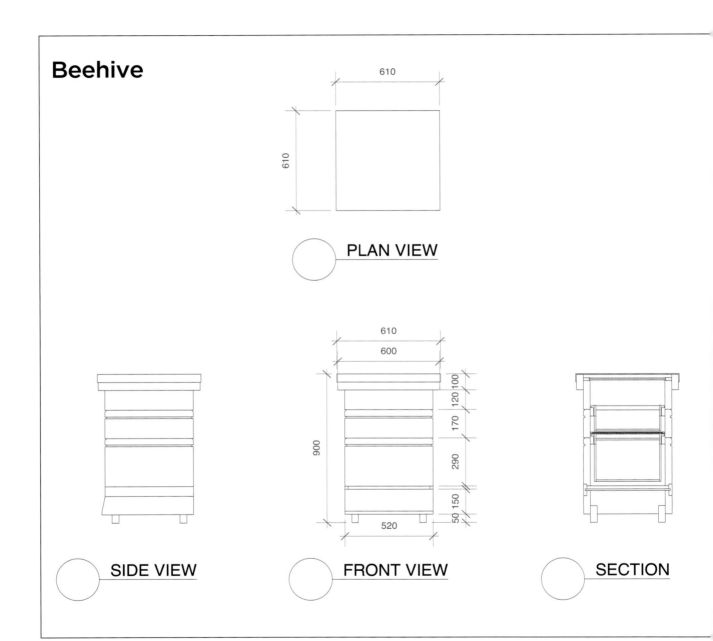

PLAN VIEW

SIDE VIEW

FRONT VIEW

SECTION

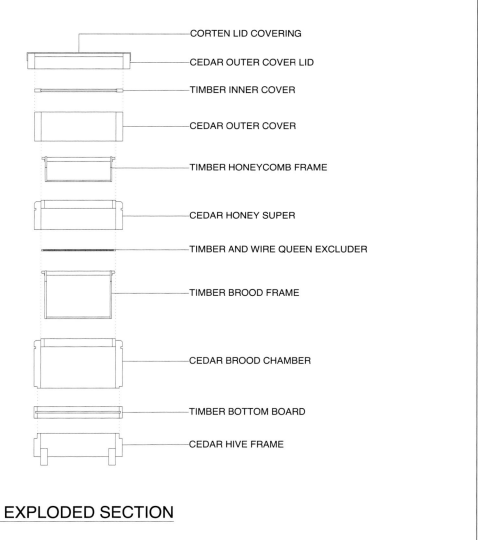

CORTEN LID COVERING

CEDAR OUTER COVER LID

TIMBER INNER COVER

CEDAR OUTER COVER

TIMBER HONEYCOMB FRAME

CEDAR HONEY SUPER

TIMBER AND WIRE QUEEN EXCLUDER

TIMBER BROOD FRAME

CEDAR BROOD CHAMBER

TIMBER BOTTOM BOARD

CEDAR HIVE FRAME

EXPLODED SECTION

Railings for cedar path

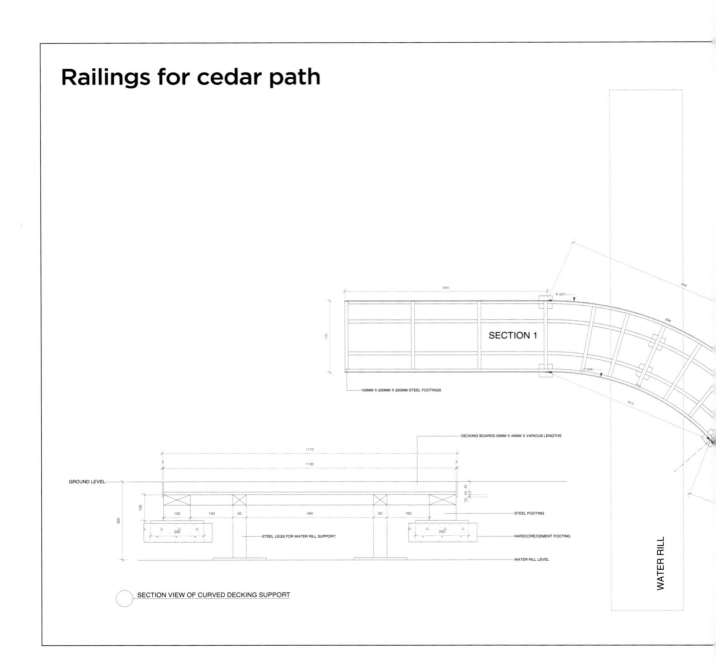

SECTION 1

100MM X 200MM X 200MM STEEL FOOTINGS

DECKING BOARDS 50MM X 40MM X VARIOUS LENGTHS

GROUND LEVEL

STEEL FOOTING

STEEL LEGS FOR WATER RILL SUPPORT

HARDCORE/CEMENT FOOTING

WATER RILL LEVEL

SECTION VIEW OF CURVED DECKING SUPPORT

WATER RILL

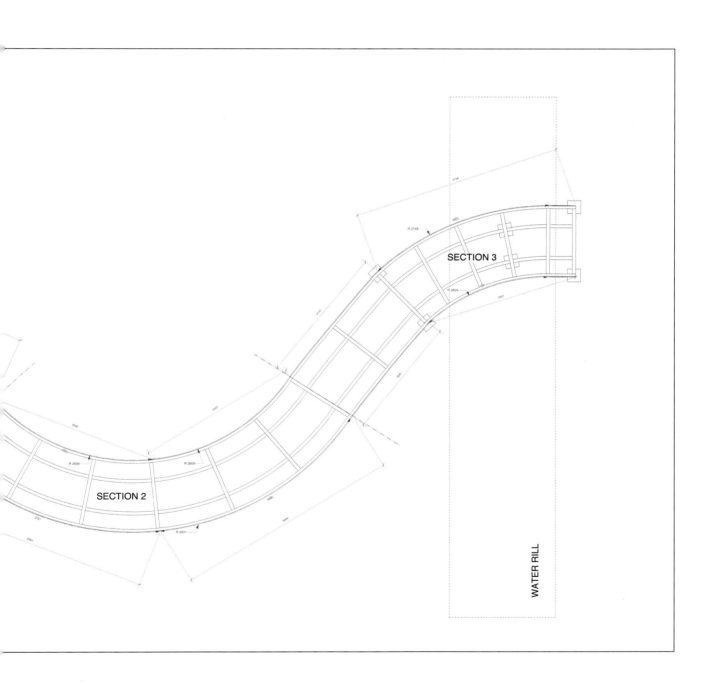

SECTION 3

SECTION 2

WATER RILL

Concrete and corten water wall

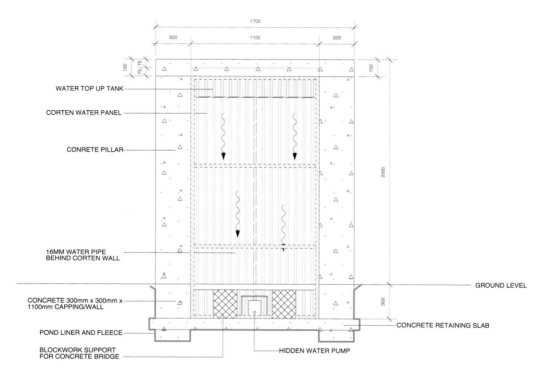

WATER TOP UP TANK

CORTEN WATER PANEL

CONRETE PILLAR

16MM WATER PIPE
BEHIND CORTEN WALL

CONCRETE 300mm x 300mm x
1100mm CAPPING/WALL

POND LINER AND FLEECE

BLOCKWORK SUPPORT
FOR CONCRETE BRIDGE

GROUND LEVEL

CONCRETE RETAINING SLAB

HIDDEN WATER PUMP

1700
300
1100
300
150
75 75
2000
300

CONCRETE AND CORTEN WATER WALL 1 - FRONT VIEW

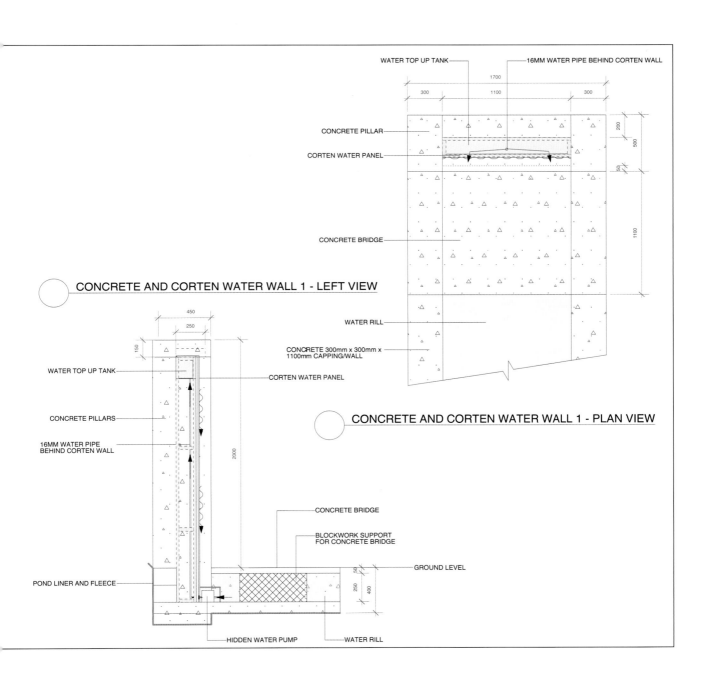

CONCRETE AND CORTEN WATER WALL 1 - LEFT VIEW

CONCRETE AND CORTEN WATER WALL 1 - PLAN VIEW

WATER TOP UP TANK — 16MM WATER PIPE BEHIND CORTEN WALL

1700
300 — 1100 — 300

200
500
50

CONCRETE PILLAR

CORTEN WATER PANEL

1100

CONCRETE BRIDGE

WATER RILL

CONCRETE 300mm x 300mm x
1100mm CAPPING/WALL

450
250
150

WATER TOP UP TANK — CORTEN WATER PANEL

CONCRETE PILLARS

16MM WATER PIPE
BEHIND CORTEN WALL

2000

CONCRETE BRIDGE

BLOCKWORK SUPPORT
FOR CONCRETE BRIDGE

GROUND LEVEL

50
250
400

POND LINER AND FLEECE

HIDDEN WATER PUMP — WATER RILL

Day 1 Building Urban Retreat at Chelsea 2015

Day 2 Building Urban Retreat at Chelsea 2015

Day 3 Building Urban Retreat at Chelsea 2015

Day 4 Building Urban Retreat at Chelsea 2015

All images: Charlie Hopper

Day 5 Building Urban Retreat at Chelsea 2015

Day 6 Building Urban Retreat at Chelsea 2015

Day 7 Building Urban Retreat at Chelsea 2015

Day 8 Building Urban Retreat at Chelsea 2015

All images: Charlie Hopper

Day 9 Building Urban Retreat at Chelsea 2015

Day 10 Building Urban Retreat at Chelsea 2015

Day 11 Building Urban Retreat at Chelsea 2015

Day 12 Building Urban Retreat at Chelsea 2015

All Images: Charlie Hopper

Day 13 Building Urban Retreat at Chelsea 2015

Day 14 Building Urban Retreat at Chelsea 2015

All images: Charlie Hopper

Day 16 Building Urban Retreat at Chelsea 2015

Day 17 Building Urban Retreat at Chelsea 2015

All images: Charlie Hopper

Press Day Urban Retreat at Chelsea 2015

Paul Smith and I show off the wonderful linings of his suits!

Angela Rippon hears about the beehive on the arbour roof

Monty Don and Paul Smith

BBC Chelsea presenter Nicky Chapm

The garden coped with the Stomp crew in the wet

Homebase Managing Director Echo Lu

With Samantha Bond, Judi Parfitt and Claire Price

Matt Baker dropped in to say Hi!

All images: Charlie Hopper

And finally . . .

Although, if I'm honest, I can't stay and watch
these gardens being taken apart, it has become
a large part of my kids' annual visit. They stay
to the very end of the show and help sell-off the
plants for charity, while I take myself to the pub
for a quiet pint. I do love the fact that most of
the plants find new homes all over the country.
Above, Amber-lily bags a verbascum for a show
visitor in 2015. I wonder where it is now?